W9-AFK-588

HEROIN
AND PRESCRIPTION OPIOIDS

BY MELISSA ABRAMOVITZ

CONTENT CONSULTANT

ANDREW HARRIS

SENIOR INVESTIGATOR
MINNEAPOLIS MEDICAL RESEARCH FOUNDATION
ASSOCIATE PROFESSOR, MEDICINE AND PSYCHOLOGY
UNIVERSITY OF MINNESOTA

An

Published by Abdo Publishing, a division of ABDO, PO Box 398166, Minneapolis, Minnesota 55439. Copyright © 2019 by Abdo Consulting Group, Inc. International copyrights reserved in all countries. No part of this book may be reproduced in any form without written permission from the publisher. Essential Library™ is a trademark and logo of Abdo Publishing.

Printed in the United States of America, North Mankato, Minnesota
022018
092018

THIS BOOK CONTAINS
RECYCLED MATERIALS

Cover Photo: Wave Break Media/iStockphoto
Interior Photos: © Alessandra De Pra/Tampa Bay Times/ZUMA, 4–5; iStockphoto, 9; Richard B. Levine/Newscom, 10; Red Line Editorial, 11, 53; Steve Heap/Shutterstock Images, 12–13; Daniel Prudek/iStockphoto, 16–17; L. Juba Photo/iStockphoto, 20; Studio Casper/iStockphoto, 22–23; Roger L. Wollenberg/UPI/Newscom, 25; Israel Leal/AP Images, 30–31; Polina Kudelkina/Shutterstock Images, 32–33; Joseph Kaczmarek/The Philadelphia Inquirer/AP Images, 34–35; Ted S. Warren/AP Images, 39; Charles Krupa/AP Images, 44; Everett Collection Historical/Alamy, 46; Amy Sancetta/ AP Images, 49; White House Photo/Alamy, 54; Dan Gleiter/PennLive.com/AP Images, 56; Mark Moran/The Citizens' Voice/AP Images, 58–59; Marlin Levison/The Star Tribune/AP Images, 64; Kevin Dietsch/UPI/Newscom, 67; Alex Milan Tracy/Sipa USA/AP Images, 69; White House/picture-alliance/ dpa/AP Images, 71; Wave Break Media/Shutterstock Images, 76; Shannon Stapleton/Reuters/ Newscom, 78–79; Brian Snyder/Reuters/Newscom, 85; Katarzyna Bialasiewicz/iStockphoto, 87; Steve Debenport/iStockphoto, 89; Craig Hudson/Charleston Gazette-Mail/AP Images, 96–97; Andrew Harnik/AP Images, 99

Editor: Alyssa Krekelberg
Series Designer: Laura Polzin

Library of Congress Control Number: 2017961352

Publisher's Cataloging-in-Publication Data
Names: Abramovitz, Melissa, author.
Title: Heroin and prescription opioids / by Melissa Abramovitz.
Description: Minneapolis, Minnesota : Abdo Publishing, 2019. | Series: Drugs in real life | Includes
        online resources and index.
Identifiers: ISBN 9781532114168 (lib.bdg.) | ISBN 9781532153990 (ebook)
Subjects: LCSH: Heroin--Juvenile literature. | Heroin abuse--Juvenile literature. |
        Opioids and opiates--Juvenile literature. | Drug control--United States--Juvenile literature.
Classification: DDC 362.299--dc23

CONTENTS

KATIE'S STORY

On the morning of April 14, 2017, 17-year-old Katie Golden told her mother that she planned to attend a drug-addiction group meeting before heading to her job at a bowling alley. Katie was a senior at Plant High School in Tampa, Florida, and she had abused marijuana since the tenth grade. She said it helped her cope with her depression and low self-esteem. Her parents, Dawn and Cliff Golden, put Katie in substance-abuse treatment programs because they knew she had a serious drug problem.

Later that day, Dawn texted Katie to find out when she needed a ride home from work. Katie never responded. Police telephoned the Goldens at approximately six o'clock in the morning to tell them an ambulance was

Cliff and Dawn Golden were heartbroken after Katie's death.

rushing Katie to the hospital. Katie had been found unconscious at the home of 17-year-old Titan Goodson, whom she dated occasionally. Titan told authorities that he and Katie had snorted heroin the previous evening. Both of them passed out. When Titan awoke, he could not rouse Katie. At 5:30 a.m. on April 15, he noticed that she felt cold and that her fingernails were blue. Someone (it isn't clear who) called 911.

Doctors managed to restart Katie's heart. But her brain had been deprived of oxygen for so long that it was permanently damaged. Katie died on April 18 after doctors took her off life support. The Hillsborough County medical examiner attributed her death to an opioid overdose.

THE HEROIN AND OPIOID EPIDEMIC

Katie's death from an opioid overdose represents an increasingly common event in America. According to the federal Centers for Disease Control and Prevention (CDC), drug overdoses are the number one cause of accidental deaths in the United States. The overdose rate quadrupled between 1999 and 2014 and continued growing through 2017. In 2015, more than 52,000 people died from overdoses.[1] More than 20,000 of these deaths involved prescription opioid pain relievers, and almost 13,000 involved heroin.[2] Heroin is an

Katie's parents don't know if the heroin that killed Katie was her first encounter with the drug. Many families affected by the heroin/prescription opioid overdose epidemic are unaware of the extent of their loved ones' drug use.

illegal opioid in the United States and cannot be prescribed by a medical professional. In July 2017, the President's Commission on Combating Drug Addiction and the Opioid Crisis issued a report stating that approximately 142 Americans were dying every day from drug overdoses in 2017. The report also revealed that "drug overdoses now kill more people than gun homicides and car crashes combined."[3]

Medical and public policy experts now refer to opioid and heroin addiction and overdose deaths as a national epidemic. The epidemic affects people of all ages and walks of life. However, researchers found that increases in opioid abuse are especially pronounced in Americans between the ages of 18 and 25 years old, in women, and in non-Hispanic Caucasians. Middletown, Ohio, is one of many places that have been devastated by the epidemic. Jack Barrett lives in Middletown and

FLORIDA HARD HIT

The opioid epidemic affects the entire United States. Some states, such as Florida, have been hit especially hard. More than 3,200 Floridians died from opioid overdoses in 2015.[4] This was approximately a 23 percent increase from 2014.[5] These increasing numbers led Governor Rick Scott to declare a public health emergency in May 2017. This action allowed Florida to receive millions of dollars in grants from the US Department of Health and Human Services. State officials used the money to ensure that first responders, such as police, paramedics, and fire department employees, throughout the state are equipped with naloxone, a drug that blocks and reverses the effects of heroin and other opioids. This drug can help save people experiencing opioid overdoses.

has a heroin addiction. "If you're young here, people just assume you're on heroin," he said.[6]

Many people who are not affected by the opioid crisis mistakenly believe that most heroin users, in particular, are impoverished, homeless, uneducated, and living in the inner cities. This was largely true in the 1960s and 1970s. The book *Dreamland* by Sam Quinones was published in 2016 and explores the opioid crisis. It points out, "People who lived in tents under underpasses used heroin" during those decades.[7] But heroin usage has spread. Today, people with heroin addictions range from suburban housewives to families in rural areas, grandparents, and teenagers living in middle- or upper-class households.

Katie Golden grew up in a middle-class home with caring, attentive parents. School was difficult for her because of her

FAMILIES SHATTERED

An increasing number of American families have been impacted by the epidemic of opioid abuse and overdoses. On March 28, 2017, 13-year-old Nathan Wylie of Dayton, Ohio, died after using a drug suspected to be heroin that belonged to his father. His father, Robert Wylie, had previously been jailed for illegal drug possession. After Nathan's death, Wylie was charged with child endangerment.

Many younger children have also died from or were successfully treated for opioid overdoses. Emergency room doctor Jennifer Plumb reported that she treated four toddlers for opioid overdoses in one night in 2017 at the Primary Children's Hospital in Salt Lake City, Utah. "These kids aren't making a choice because they are trying to get high on a substance," Plumb stated. "It's that the pills are everywhere."[8]

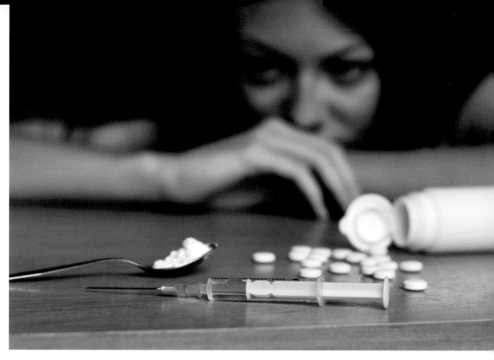

The heroin crisis has hit people from all walks of life.

depression and attention deficit hyperactivity disorder. Katie had planned to attend Eastern Florida State College after she finished high school and wanted to become a social worker. Her parents described her as a kind person. They also noted that Katie felt like she didn't fit in with her peers.

Her parents thought feeling isolated contributed to Katie's drug abuse. They took her to counselors and didn't allow her to have enough money to buy drugs. They thought these measures were helping, and Katie even passed a drug test the day before her death.

EDUCATION AND COMPASSION

Dawn and Cliff channeled their grief over their daughter's death into educating others about the dangers of heroin and other addictive drugs. One thing the Goldens stress is that people who have mental health issues, like Katie did, have an increased risk of using illegal drugs. Such people rarely seek help because of the stigma and shame associated with both mental illness and drug addiction. The Goldens are working with a group called Changing Minds Tampa to try to reduce this stigma and shame.

Medical, criminal justice, and social policy experts agree that drastic measures are needed to stem the tide of ruined lives, shattered families, crime, and other consequences of abuse and overdoses of heroin and other opioids. Government officials

Actor Philip Seymour Hoffman died of a drug overdose involving heroin in 2014.

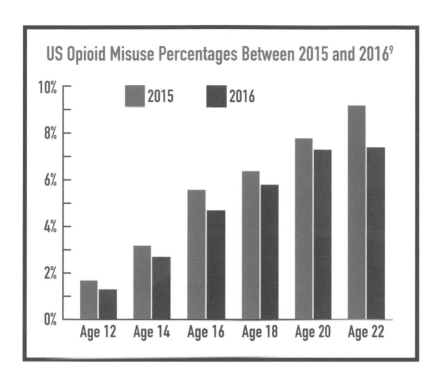

US Opioid Misuse Percentages Between 2015 and 2016[9]

and public health agencies are ramping up education about the opioid/heroin epidemic, promoting new laws that restrict access to these drugs, expanding addiction treatment, and going after drug dealers to quickly address the drug abuses and overdoses that are plaguing the United States.

CHAPTER TWO

WHAT ARE OPIOIDS?

Opioids are a class of drugs used to relieve severe physical pain. They are also known as narcotics. Legal opioids include oxycodone, morphine, hydrocodone, and fentanyl. People need a doctor's prescription to buy these drugs. Heroin is an illegal opioid that has no approved medical uses. It's illegal to make, sell, and use heroin in the United States.

Opioids such as heroin are made from opium, a milky substance found in seedpods that grow in opium poppy plants. Opium contains three opioid chemicals: morphine, codeine, and thebaine. Morphine

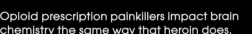

Opioid prescription painkillers impact brain chemistry the same way that heroin does.

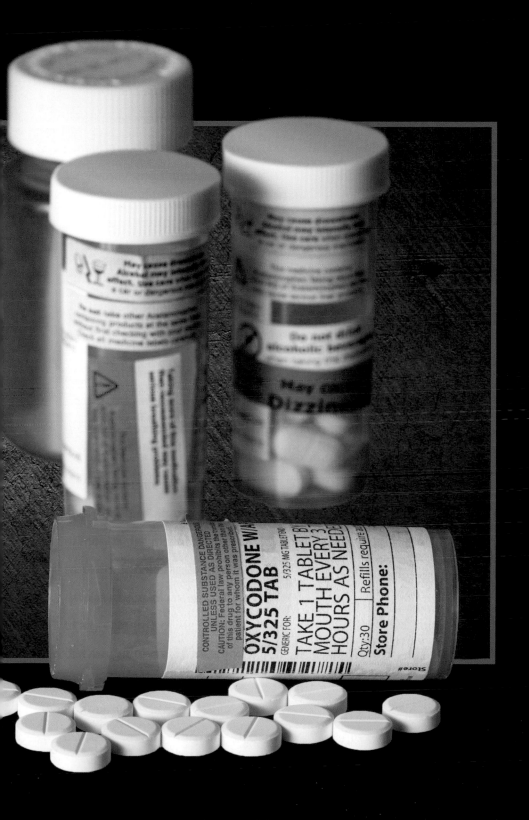

is the most powerful of these substances and is most commonly used to make opioid drugs. Opioid drugs can be made from the ingredients extracted from opium poppy seedpods, or they can be made synthetically.

Synthetic opioids have chemical structures that are similar to the natural substances found in opium. However,

Heroin is one of the fastest-acting opioids. It brings a quick rush of euphoria.

synthetic opioids are made in a laboratory. Fentanyl, carfentanil, and methadone are all synthetic opioids. All opioids can cause euphoria, which is a "high" that gives users a strong sense of well-being. Opioids also relieve pain and anxiety, slow heart rate and breathing, and cause drowsiness. All opioids can be addictive in people prone to addiction.

HISTORY OF OPIUM

People have known about the euphoric and pain-relieving qualities of opium since around 3400 BCE. But several discoveries starting in the early 1800s CE led to the widespread use of opium derivatives as medications. In approximately 1805, a German pharmacist's apprentice, Friedrich Sertürner, isolated the chemical that gave opium its power. He named it morphine, after Morpheus, the Greek god of dreams. Morphine was soon used as a drug to help people sleep and to relieve pain. Military doctors began administering it to injured soldiers in wars such as the

American Civil War (1861–1865). Tens of thousands of soldiers and others who used morphine became addicted to it.

In 1853, Dr. Alexander Wood of Scotland invented the hypodermic needle. The needle made it possible to inject drugs into veins. This method allows the drug's effects to spread through the bloodstream much faster than when using other methods, such as taking the drug orally or putting it on the skin's surface. Morphine was the first drug to be injected intravenously. This method, when coupled with morphine, offered much quicker pain relief along with the drug's other effects. But the dangers of injecting drugs into the bloodstream also became apparent. Large amounts of morphine injected intravenously can slow an individual's

THE JOY PLANT

The first recorded use of opium was in Mesopotamia, in what is modern-day Iraq. There, the Sumerians built one of the world's earliest civilizations. Historians believe the Sumerians grew the first opium poppies in approximately 3400 BCE. They called the poppy *hul gil*, which translates to "joy plant." From there, the practice of growing opium poppies spread throughout the world. Today, opium poppies are usually grown in warm, dry climates.

Historians believe the ancient Egyptians also made the goopy substance inside the poppy seedpods into a drug to treat specific illnesses. These drugs were used to lessen physical and emotional distress and to help people sleep. Historians also believe people in some ancient civilizations knew that opioids were addictive and could be fatal.

Some opium poppies are cultivated to be used in making medical opioids.

breathing so much that he or she becomes unconscious or dies of an overdose.

HEROIN ARRIVES

The fact that some people become addicted to morphine led chemists and pharmacists to search for a similar drug that was less likely to lead to addictive behavior. The British physician Dr. Charles Alder Wright first synthesized diacetylmorphine from

morphine in 1874. In 1898, German chemist Heinrich Dreser renamed the substance heroin. The word *heroin* is derived from the Greek word *hērōs*. The ancient Greeks used the term to refer to half-human, half-god beings with extraordinary powers. The term also means a protector or defender. Dreser chose this name because of the euphoric feeling the drug produced and because of its miraculous ability to reduce pain, anxiety, and other

OPIUM IN THE UNITED STATES

Opium and morphine were widely cultivated and used in places such as India and China in the 1800s. Chinese immigrants came to the United States during this period to either work on the growing railroad system or to capitalize on the California Gold Rush. Some immigrants brought their practice of smoking opium with them. They set up numerous opium dens in places such as San Francisco's Chinatown. The US government soon outlawed opium dens to prevent this habit of smoking opium from spreading in America, but the use of morphine in medicines such as cough syrups spread.

unpleasant conditions such as headaches and coughs.

Dreser worked for a pharmaceutical company in Germany that began marketing the drug as a nonaddictive remedy for colds, coughs, asthma, tuberculosis, and other ailments in 1898. At first, doctors and the general public thought heroin was not addictive, so it was sold without needing a prescription. But many people who used heroin to alleviate pain or to treat their addictions to morphine or codeine soon became addicted to heroin.

Heroin abuse and addiction became a widespread problem in the United States in the early 1900s. By 1924, approximately 200,000 Americans were addicted to heroin.[1] Many of them engaged in criminal activities to help finance their habit. In 1924, this led Congress to update the Harrison Narcotics Tax Act of 1914. The updated law made it illegal to import, manufacture, sell, and use heroin in the United States. Heroin use declined in the 1930s and 1940s. However, illegal heroin use increased in the

1950s, 1960s, and 1970s as more and more people tried heroin and developed addictions. Heroin use reached new highs in the late 1990s and early 2000s, and prescription opioid abuse also increased dramatically.

HOW ARE HEROIN AND PRESCRIPTION OPIOIDS SOLD AND USED?

Today, most heroin comes from Asia, South and Central America, or Mexico. Heroin from Asia and Latin America is usually sold as a white or brownish-colored powder. Heroin from Mexico is usually a black, sticky goop known as black tar heroin. Most heroin is mixed with other drugs such as fentanyl or cocaine, or with sugar, starch, or powdered milk. Mixing fentanyl or cocaine with heroin leads to a more intense high. Dealers mix heroin with sugar, starch, or powdered milk so they can make more money by selling a smaller amount of heroin. Users do not know the heroin's purity when they buy it. The purer the heroin, the stronger its effects. This unknown quantity makes it easier for people to overdose or experience other adverse effects.

Heroin can be injected into a vein or under the skin, smoked, or snorted. These methods of taking the drug all bring fast euphoria. However, injection into a vein brings the fastest high. The high achieved from snorting heroin takes longer for the user to feel. However, it can last longer than the high that occurs with other methods of administration.

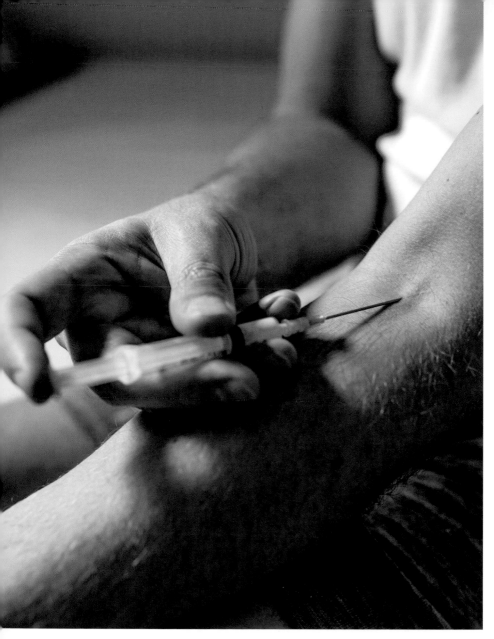

Intravenous drug use can cause bacterial infections.

Unlike heroin, prescription opioids such as hydrocodone and oxycodone usually come in pill form. They are often prescribed by doctors after a person undergoes surgery or has another type of severe pain. Some prescription opioid pills, such as OxyContin, contain a special coating that allows the drug to be released gradually over 12 hours. Another prescription opioid called fentanyl comes in the form of a skin patch that slowly releases the drug over a period of time.

Problems with abuse begin when people keep using prescription opioids when the medical need for them stops. Such individuals, seeking to bring on a sense of euphoria, may take more pills at a time than prescribed. Or they may crush the pills, mix them with liquid, and inject the mixture into a vein for a quicker, more intense high. Others start abusing prescription opioids when a family member or friend shares the drugs with someone with no medical need. Once someone abuses these drugs, he or she may want more pills than a doctor will prescribe. Such individuals may start buying prescription opioids on the street.

HOW FAST IS FAST?

Heroin works fast and brings a quick rush of euphoria, also known as a "high." This is why many people start using it. But how fast is fast? That depends on how heroin is taken. Injecting it intravenously—directly into a vein—brings a rush of euphoria in seven to eight seconds. The rush starts five to eight minutes after heroin is injected into a muscle. Smoking or snorting it generally gives users a rush in 10 to 15 minutes. However, some users report that smoking it brings a high within just a few minutes.[2]

CHAPTER THREE

IMPACTS ON THE BRAIN AND BODY

After heroin or prescription opioids enter the body, the drug is transported across the blood-brain barrier. The blood-brain barrier consists of tightly packed cells inside blood vessels that do not allow certain harmful substances to enter the brain. Cells in this barrier do not perceive opioids to be a threat. Once opioids are inside the brain, enzymes eventually convert them into morphine. Morphine, like other opioids, acts by binding to opioid receptors on neurons, or nerve cells. Receptors absorb

The white powder form of heroin is commonly found in the eastern United States.

and respond to brain chemicals or to substances administered externally. Scientists find that many people with addictions have fewer-than-normal numbers of opioid receptors, both before and after the addiction is developed. The lack of opioid receptors may be why people prone to addiction feel a need to flood the brain with externally administered opioids.

Until the 1970s, scientists didn't understand how heroin and other opioids affect the brain. But in 1974, neurobiologist Solomon H. Snyder and his associates at the Johns Hopkins University School of Medicine in Maryland discovered that the brains of humans and other mammals contain specific opioid receptors.

Snyder's work caused many scientists to wonder why the brain contains specific receptors for a substance (opium) that people didn't know about or use until approximately 5,000 years ago. According to neuroscientist Richard F. Thompson, "Only one answer seemed possible: the brain must make or use chemical substances very similar to opium."[1] Researchers John Hughes and Hans Kosterlitz at the University of Aberdeen in Scotland confirmed this

CHILDHOOD TRAUMA AND OPIOID RECEPTORS

Research indicates there is a biological basis for childhood abuse or neglect leading to later drug addiction. The brains of abused or neglected children produce less-than-normal amounts of the natural endorphins that diminish physical and emotional pain. This leads to fewer opioid receptors in the brain than is normal.

In 2003, Solomon H. Snyder, *left*, received the National Medal of Science for his work on the brain's neurotransmitters, receptors, and pathways.

theory in 1975. They found a substance in the brains of pigs that they called enkephalin, which is a naturally produced opioid. Enkephalin acts like morphine; it attaches to the same types of neuron receptors. Other scientists then discovered other naturally occurring opioids in the brain. The group name for these substances is endorphins.

ADOLESCENTS AND ADDICTION

Drug and alcohol abuse during adolescence is one of the strongest risk factors for later drug addiction. Dr. John Knight of the Center for Adolescent Substance Abuse Research at Boston Children's Hospital explains, "When people start using at younger ages, the changes in brain structure and function are very, very pronounced. If we could only get kids to postpone their first drink or their first use of drugs, we could greatly diminish the prevalence of addiction in the U.S."[2]

One reason drug abuse in adolescents strongly influences addiction risk is that the brain is still developing. The damage drugs do on the developing prefrontal cortex area of the brain can be especially devastating and long lasting. This area plays a big role in decision-making and self-control.

A National Institute on Drug Abuse (NIDA) report asserts that cutting down on adolescents' use of drugs would have dramatic effects: "If we can prevent young people from experimenting with drugs, we can prevent drug addiction."[3]

Later on, scientists discovered that there are three main types of opioid receptors: mu, delta, and kappa. Opioids act mostly on mu receptors. When a drug binds to and activates these receptors, it starts a series of communications between neurons. The ultimate result is that a large amount of the neurotransmitter dopamine, which causes feelings of pleasure, is released. Dopamine floods into the reward, or pleasure pathway, areas of the brain. Areas in the cerebral cortex, limbic system, and brain stem make up this pathway. Dopamine causes the euphoria and the other effects, such as pain relief, that users of opioids experience.

Besides euphoria and pain relief, short-term effects of heroin and prescription opioids include drowsiness, slowed breathing and heart rate, constricted pupils, nausea, vomiting, flushing of the skin, dry mouth, and a heavy feeling in the arms and legs. Itching may also occur. The user stays drowsy for several hours and often cannot think clearly. This allows him or her to disconnect from reality, which is the primary reason most people take heroin and similar drugs, according to many experts and drug abusers. Addiction expert Dr. Gabor Maté, for instance, states in his book *In the Realm of Hungry Ghosts* that all his patients use mind-altering drugs to deaden the emotional pain in their lives.

OVERDOSES

The effects of heroin and prescription opioids on breathing and heart rate come from the drug's influence on parts of the brain stem. This area at the back of the brain controls automatic functions such as heart rate and breathing. Such effects are also responsible for the risks of overdose and death. A large enough dose slows the user's breathing and heart rate so much that the individual goes into a coma or dies. Even if the person lives, slowed breathing can cause less oxygen to travel to body organs and cells. This can permanently damage these organs, including the brain.

Some people with heroin or prescription opioid addictions die from overdoses or other adverse effects. Symptoms of an overdose are slowed breathing, blue lips and fingernails, clammy

COUNTERACTING OVERDOSES

Overdose deaths from heroin and prescription opioids can be prevented. A drug called naloxone reverses the effects of overdoses. Naloxone binds to opioid receptors in the brain so these drugs cannot activate those receptors. It basically works like a baseball player who pushes another player off a base and takes the other player's place. Public health officials and lawmakers have taken steps to expand access to naloxone. In 2014, the US Food and Drug Administration approved the naloxone auto-injector Evzio. Family members and other people without medical training can use Evzio to reverse heroin overdoses. Many police and other first responders now carry Evzio or other forms of naloxone.

skin, convulsions, or a coma. Many times, the first indication of an overdose occurs when a user becomes unconscious. According to Dr. Joseph C. Mancini, "The ability of opioids to consistently and predictably shut down the respiratory drive [breathing] is the reason we are now in the midst of this epidemic of sudden death caused by opioids."[4]

One reason for overdoses is that users never know how pure a street drug like heroin is. Many dealers now add the opioid fentanyl to heroin. The intense high this creates makes users want to buy even more of the drug. Fentanyl is very easy and inexpensive to make.

It is also extremely dangerous. A dose of fentanyl the size of a grain of sand can be fatal. Thus, even small amounts of fentanyl mixed into heroin raise the overdose danger. In September 2016, law enforcement officials found carfentanil, which is an opioid even stronger than fentanyl, in a batch of heroin. It caused nine overdose deaths in Cincinnati, Ohio.[5]

People who abuse prescription opioids often overdose because they develop tolerance. This means they need more and more of the drug to experience the same euphoric effects. But too much can result in an overdose. In other cases, crushing pills like OxyContin that are meant to release over 12 hours causes the entire dose to become immediately effective. This large dose can cause an overdose.

EFFECTS IN LONG-TERM USERS

Longtime heroin and prescription opioid users can experience a variety of physical and psychological problems. Common effects include insomnia, constipation, heart disease, liver disease, kidney disease, breathing problems, and lung diseases such as pneumonia and tuberculosis. Dizziness and drowsiness from these drugs commonly lead users to fall and break bones. Neurological damage often leads to heightened sensitivity to pain and to mood swings and memory problems. Researchers note that prescription opioids such as Percocet and Vicodin that also contain the painkiller acetaminophen are especially likely to cause liver or kidney failure. High doses of acetaminophen are proven to be a common cause of these problems.

In 2015, the highest heroin overdose rates occurred in men aged 25 to 44. The death rate from overdose was 13.2 men per 100,000 in the US population in this age group.[6]

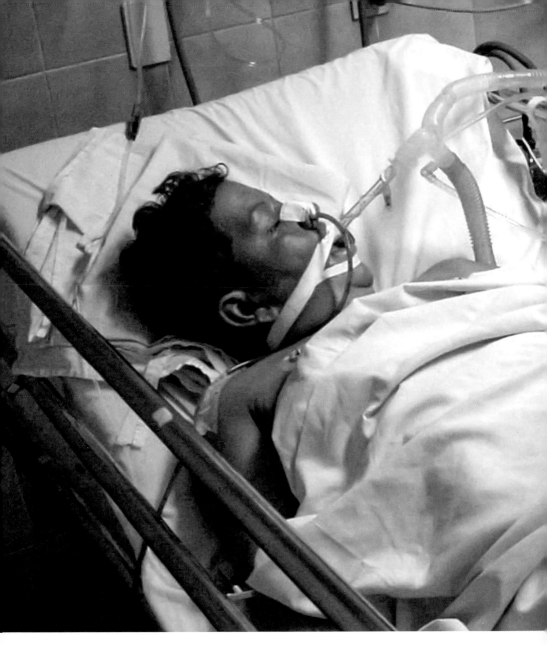

Drug use is stressful on the human body and forces some addicted people into hospitals.

Other common long-term effects of heroin and prescription opioids include a disruption of women's menstrual cycles and sexual dysfunction in men. Psychological effects from long-term

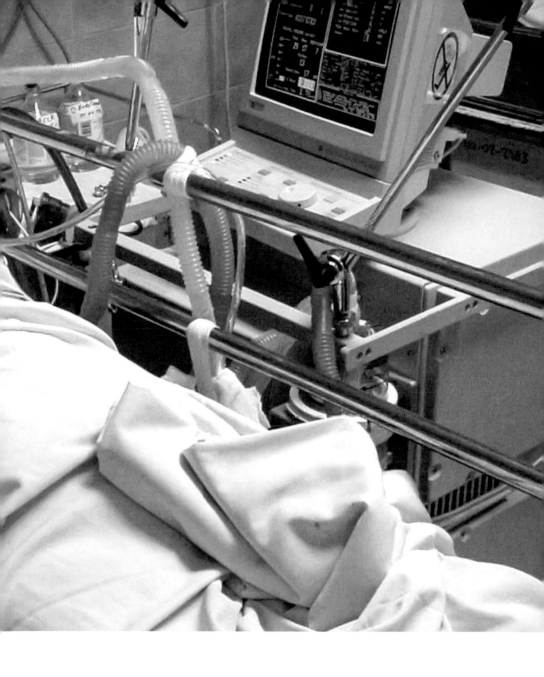

use often include depression, delusions, paranoia, and an antisocial personality.

HOW OPIOIDS AFFECT THE BRAIN

DRUG-FREE CONDITIONS

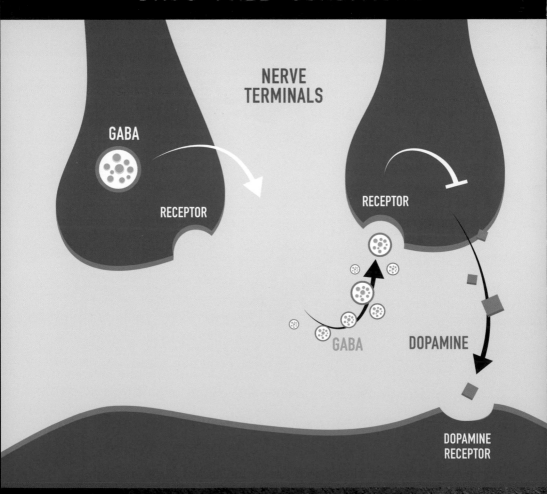

NERVE
TERMINALS

GABA

RECEPTOR

RECEPTOR

GABA

DOPAMINE

DOPAMINE
RECEPTOR

When opioids bind to receptors, they repress the neurotransmitter gamma-aminobutyric acid (GABA). Under typical circumstances, GABA lowers the amount of dopamine released. When opioids repress GABA, it leads to increased dopamine release.

OPIOIDS IN THE BRAIN

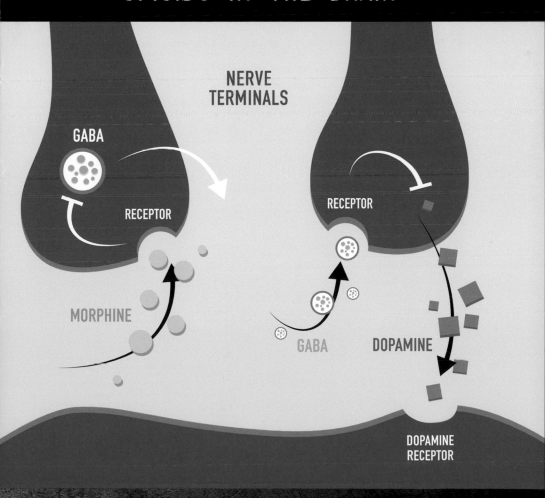

NERVE TERMINALS

GABA

RECEPTOR

RECEPTOR

MORPHINE

GABA

DOPAMINE

DOPAMINE RECEPTOR

RISKS
AND EFFECTS

Addiction is one of the most serious problems associated with opioids. A variety of biological, environmental, and social factors interact to cause addiction. One biological factor is genetics. Certain types of gene mutations, or abnormalities, raise the risk of developing addiction. Genetic factors account for approximately one-half of an individual's risk. This is why the tendency for addiction runs in families. Children of people with addictions do not necessarily develop addictions themselves, but they do have a greater-than-normal risk.

When people die from opioid overdoses, many families are left confused and upset.

In Loving Memory of Tommy Shannon Jr.

STOP the HEROIN

07-20-84 •

People with certain personality traits and behaviors are also at higher risk for addiction. People who are impulsive, seek thrills, or need constant reassurance or comfort from others are at high risk. In addition, people who suffer from mental illnesses are also at a higher risk for developing an addiction. Most people with addictions start using drugs that soothe emotional pain because they didn't learn to cope with distressing situations in healthy ways. For example, Lindsey Greinke became addicted to prescription opioids because Vicodin relieved her depression and anxiety when a doctor first prescribed it for a neck injury when she was 12 years old. "I basically thought to myself, 'Wow, this is exactly what I'm looking for,'" she later stated. "This completely numbs the pain, not just physically, but emotionally."[1]

Addiction experts find that one of the most powerful risk factors for later drug addiction is abusing alcohol or drugs during adolescence. For example, ex-National Basketball Association (NBA) player Chris Herren began smoking marijuana and abusing alcohol during his freshman year of high school. He soon moved on to cocaine, OxyContin, and heroin. Herren had another powerful risk factor for addiction—being an athlete. The pressure on athletes to power through pain and play while injured leads many to become addicted to opioids. In fact, almost one-half of the players on Herren's legendary high school basketball team in Fall River, Massachusetts, became addicted to heroin.

Experiencing physical, sexual, or emotional abuse or neglect during childhood also raises the risk of substance addiction. The Adverse Childhood Experiences study found that one adverse childhood experience, such as being abused, increased the risk of substance addiction dramatically. Growing up with parents or other family members who abuse drugs is also a powerful risk factor, as is having easy access to addictive drugs. The more risk factors an individual has, the greater the chance of developing an addiction.

THE POWER OF ADDICTION

Herren lost his NBA career because of his addiction to heroin and other drugs. Now sober, he shares the ways in which his addiction took over his life. Herren notes that after his first child was born, he left his wife and baby at the hospital to get high. In 2001, his family and fans eagerly awaited his debut with the Boston Celtics inside the Fleet Center arena. But Herren stood outside in the rain, waiting for his drug dealer to show up. After that, he regularly shot up heroin before games. At one point, he was spending thousands of dollars per month on drugs.

CHARACTERISTICS OF ADDICTION

Addiction occurs when a user develops psychological and physical dependence on a drug. One characteristic of addiction is tolerance. This means the user's body gets used to the drug, and increasingly larger doses are required to achieve the same effect. Other characteristics are withdrawal and cravings. If a person with an addiction stops taking the drug, withdrawal occurs within 24 to 48 hours. Symptoms include restlessness, insomnia, bone and muscle pain, nausea, vomiting, diarrhea, chills, and possibly even death unless the addicted person receives medical attention. Opioids such as heroin cause the most unpleasant withdrawal effects among drugs, according to addiction expert Dr. Joseph Mancini. This makes quitting very difficult. Deon, a man who recovered from his heroin addiction, said withdrawal felt like he "was dying in every awful way you could think of, all at once. Pain in all my bones, throwing up, chills, and I couldn't sleep for days."[2]

The power of heroin addiction is illustrated by the fact that studies show up to 91 percent of addicted people start using the drug again after completing addiction treatment. One study found that 59 percent started using again within one week after completing treatment.[4]

THE DRUG'S CONTROL

Avoiding withdrawal symptoms and fulfilling drug cravings lead people with addictions to view heroin or other opioids as the most important thing in their lives. As addiction specialist Dr. Gabor Maté explains, "People jeopardize their lives for the sake of making the moment livable. Nothing sways them from the habit—not illness, not the sacrifice of love and relationships, not the loss of all earthly goods, not the crushing of their dignity, not the fear of dying. The drive is that relentless."[3]

These drugs' control over a person's body occurs because of changes in the person's brain. The ongoing release of dopamine and other neurotransmitters that impact the brain's motivation, memory, and pleasure and reward centers cause these changes. For instance, the prefrontal cortex shrinks after long-term heroin and prescription opioid abuse. This disrupts an addicted person's ability to regulate and control behavior, respond to stress, and make decisions. A structure in the midbrain called the striatum starts coordinating addictive behaviors based on the addicted person's intense desire for the drug. For example, logic and self-control are overruled by desire and the compulsion to seek and ingest the drug.

Many states are seeing a rise in opioid overdose deaths.

IS ADDICTION CAUSED BY PHYSIOLOGY?

It may seem that something within heroin and prescription opioids is controlling an addicted person's compulsions to seek and ingest them. However, researchers have discovered that addiction is caused by factors within people prone to addiction, not within drugs like heroin. These factors include genetics, motivation, experiences, and coping mechanisms. As psychiatrist Lance Dodes explains, "Addiction is a human problem that resides in people, not in the drug or in the drug's capacity to produce physical effects."[5] This is why not everyone who uses opioids becomes addicted. Indeed, doctors estimate that only 23 percent of the people who use heroin become addicted.[6]

Experts like Dodes emphasize that only those with certain risk factors that predispose them to addiction become addicted. For instance, one risk factor is inheriting gene mutations that result in fewer opioid receptors in the brain's reward pathways than normal. Such individuals tend to rely on external sources of dopamine such as heroin and other opioids to soothe anxiety because taking these drugs produces more dopamine than the brain produces internally. Those who lack enough dopamine receptors need greater amounts of dopamine to give them feelings of pleasure. So rather than developing more productive ways of coping, such as exercising or talking to a friend, addiction-prone people tend to turn to external sources of dopamine to make them feel good when they feel stressed or unhappy.

LIFE WITH ADDICTION

Opioid addiction affects every aspect of an addicted person's life. School performance, personal relationships, and everything else take a back seat to finding and using these drugs. Some people with addiction manage to function relatively normally for a while. However, they often start missing school or work and do a poor job when present because of drowsiness and other effects of the drug. For example, Matt Schoonover of Columbus, Ohio, started using prescription opioids in college and dropped out of school. He began working for caterers and became what is known as a functional addict. He could work, but he relied on numerous doses of pills to get through each day. However, once he started using heroin, he could no longer work.

CRIME AND ADDICTION

Dr. Gabor Maté works in an inner-city addiction clinic in Canada. He describes how many patients look for opportunities to steal wherever they may be. One longtime patient, Mike, stole an electronic device from Maté's desk. Maté had left Mike alone in his office for approximately 20 seconds. When confronted about the theft, Mike replied, "It was there on your desk. What could I do?"

Maté notes in his book *In the Realm of Hungry Ghosts*, "I naively believed that this man, who once made me a finely worked wood carving to express his gratitude, could be trusted. Perhaps he could be trusted, but his addiction could not."[7]

Many people addicted to heroin and prescription opioids cannot hold a job because they make accessing and using the drug the highest priority in their lives. They may turn to crime to get the money they need to buy the drug they crave. Some people are arrested numerous times, and they acquire a criminal record. If an addicted person is convicted of a felony, he or she has trouble finding jobs because employers are hesitant to hire someone with a criminal record, even if the individual is in recovery and is trying to start a new life.

Many people with addictions also become homeless because their focus on getting drugs hurts their ability to hold down a steady job, or because they have spent much of their money on drugs. Tracey Helton Mitchell became homeless after becoming addicted to heroin while in college. In her book *The Big Fix*, she writes about going through withdrawal "while I was living on the sidewalk, twitching and puking into the gutter."[8]

IS ADDICTION A DISEASE?

Although experts agree that addiction is a major problem, controversies exist about what addiction is. Most modern experts, including the American Medical Association, American Society of Addiction Medicine, and National Institutes of Health, believe addiction is a brain disease. The National Institute on Drug Abuse (NIDA) describes it as "a chronic, relapsing brain disease that is characterized by compulsive drug seeking and use, despite harmful consequences."[9] The National Center on Addiction and Substance Abuse (CASA) explains that the disease of addiction comes from brain changes in areas responsible for "reward, motivation, learning, judgement, and memory."[10]

Psychiatrist David Sack believes three main factors make addiction a disease. First, people with addictions are prone to relapse after recovery, just as people with diseases such as cancer are. Second, people with one type of addiction often develop other addictions. For example, an individual addicted to heroin is likely to become addicted to cigarettes. Sack believes this is because different types of addiction are subtypes of one disease. Third, medications can effectively treat drug addictions and other diseases. Anti-addiction medications reduce cravings and block the effects of addictive drugs.

However, medications are not usually effective in changing habitual behaviors.

The theory that addiction is a disease follows the tendency in psychiatry to blame a disease process, rather than a person, for mental and behavior problems. In fact, agencies such as the National Council on Alcoholism and Drug Dependence and the National Center on Addiction and Substance Abuse encourage addicted individuals and their families to embrace this view because research suggests it may diminish the associated stigma. If someone has a disease, he or she cannot help having it. This

Serenity Place is a treatment center in New Hampshire. The organization's Safe Station Program encourages people with addictions to go to a fire station and ask for help.

in turn makes some addicted people more willing to seek treatment and some families more willing to support an addicted person's recovery.

Other experts argue that addiction is a learned behavior or habit. One reason neuroscientist Marc Lewis believes this is that many people with addictions defeat addiction simply by choosing to overcome it, with little or no treatment. With diseases such as cancer, choosing to get rid of the disease does not make it go away. Lewis believes "addiction is a habit, which like other habits, gets entrenched through a decrease in self-control." He agrees that addiction involves brain changes in the part of the brain he calls "the neural circuitry of desire."[11] But he emphasizes that any type of learning, including learning

IS ADDICTION A LEARNED HABIT?

Neuroscience journalist Maia Szalavitz believes addiction is a learned behavior, not a disease. She states that people with substance addiction learn to behave in ways that help them diminish stress. Indeed, most addicted people begin using drugs to diminish stress. Once addicted, they continue using to avoid the stress of withdrawal. These behaviors result from and cause certain brain changes. But as Szalavitz notes, anything that makes people feel pleasure activates changes in the same brain regions that underlie addiction.

Studies by James P. Burkitt and Larry J. Young at Emory University in Georgia support this theory. They found that changes in the prefrontal cortex and striatum that occur when humans fall in love are similar to the changes that occur in addiction. "Simply changing the brain doesn't make addiction a disease," Szalavitz writes.[12]

the habit of drug abuse, results in changes in the structure, function, and connections of neurons in the brain. However, Lewis notes that this does not make it a disease. Instead, he equates addiction to other self-destructive habits such as adultery or violence.

Proponents of both viewpoints agree that a variety of genetic, physiological, and environmental factors cause addiction. Both viewpoints are also consistent with the fact that overcoming an addiction and staying sober is extremely difficult. Not only must people with addictions endure withdrawal, but they must also develop new ways of coping with life's challenges. As Mitchell puts it, "By focusing on little achievements, I incrementally build an entirely new existence for myself."[13]

SOCIAL EFFECTS

The damaging effects of heroin and prescription opioid abuse and addiction extend beyond individual users. Families and society are profoundly affected. As Dr. Nora D. Volkow of NIDA states, "The medical and social consequences of drug use—such as hepatitis, HIV/AIDS, fetal effects, crime, violence, and disruptions in family, workplace, and educational environments—have a devastating impact on society and cost billions of dollars each year."[1]

HEROIN AND PRESCRIPTION OPIOIDS AFFECT COMMUNITIES

Heroin and prescription opioid addictions have devastated many communities. Small to medium-sized towns in states such as Ohio and West Virginia have been hit especially hard.

Bags of heroin were seized by authorities in Cleveland, Ohio, in 2010.

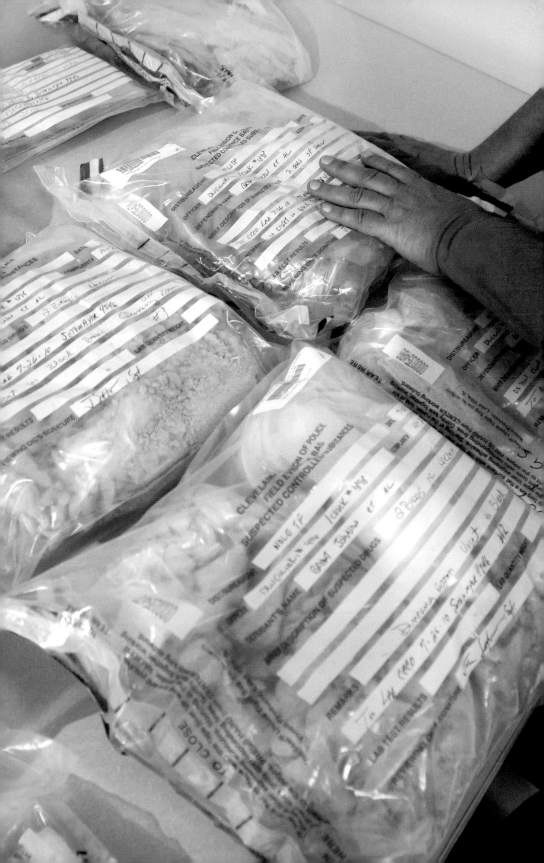

Middletown and Portsmouth in Ohio are two such communities. Crime rates have skyrocketed as many people with addictions steal money and goods to feed their habit. Home burglaries and shoplifting from stores are rampant. Local residents have told journalists that people with addictions steal Christmas presents from their own families and from strangers. People with addictions have also been known to forge checks and steal credit cards to pay for drugs. Police in Portsmouth report that desperate addicted people routinely rip apart and steal copper wire from the outdoor condensers on air-conditioning units and sell the wire to metal recyclers.

The increasing number of prescription opioid and heroin overdoses also impacts communities. Finding people with addictions passed out in their cars or elsewhere has become commonplace in the United States. A fire captain in Middletown told investigators that he and other first responders see the same addicted people overdosing again and again. Every time, he warns them that it is important to go to a hospital to begin treatment.

In 2015, West Virginia experienced the highest overdose death rate in the country, with approximately 41 deaths per 100,000 people. New Hampshire ranked second with approximately 34 deaths per 100,000 people; Ohio and Kentucky tied for third with approximately 30 deaths per 100,000 people.[2]

ECONOMIC EFFECTS

Expenses from treating overdoses are straining local

budgets. Cities pay first responders' salaries and the other expenses of sending them to respond to these emergencies. They also buy Narcan, a form of naloxone, and other tools used to save the lives of people with addictions. Since few addicted people have money, community taxpayers end up bearing these costs. For example, Middletown's annual budget is $29 million. In 2016, the city spent $1.2 million responding to 532 instances of opioid overdoses. Sending paramedics to administer one dose of Narcan costs the city $1,104. In the first six months of 2017, first responders had made 598 overdose runs.[3] The city council admitted in 2017 that it might need to lay off city employees in other departments because of these rising costs. Some residents have stated that taxpayer dollars should not be

COMMUNITIES IMPACTED

Investigators have studied the dramatic rise in opioid and heroin abuse in Middletown, Ohio, because the town "offers a lesson in the speed and power with which addiction can sabotage a community," explains journalist Emily de La Bruyère.[4]

The epidemic affects Middletown residents in every walk of life. People addicted to heroin or prescription opioids can range from teachers and doctors to construction workers and businesspeople. One mother of three notes that "everyone I know is on heroin."[5] Heroin addiction pushed this mother into poverty. Eating a free breakfast at a local church became an integral part of her life. But she knows she is better off than her neighbor, who lost two children to heroin overdoses in 2017. Indeed, most families in Middletown are directly impacted by opioids. Resident Terri Fugate's son, sister, and boyfriend are all recovering from heroin addictions.

wasted on reviving people who overdose on drugs. Others argue that people with addictions deserve compassion because they cannot help their behavior.

Federal and state governments also use taxpayer dollars to rescue people who have overdosed and to pay for their treatment, incarceration, and/or living expenses. Each year, these costs total billions of dollars. A 2017 report by health economics professor Dr. Richard Frank of the Harvard Medical School estimates that the yearly cost of treating opioid addiction may reach $220 billion by 2026 if recent trends continue.[6]

SOCIAL EFFECTS ON CHILDREN

The social and economic effects of opioid abuse extend to users being unable to care for their children. Children who grow up with addicted parents have an increased risk for abuse and neglect. In addition, these children are at high risk of becoming addicted to drugs. Many such children drop out of or perform poorly in school. Many girls also face unplanned pregnancies,

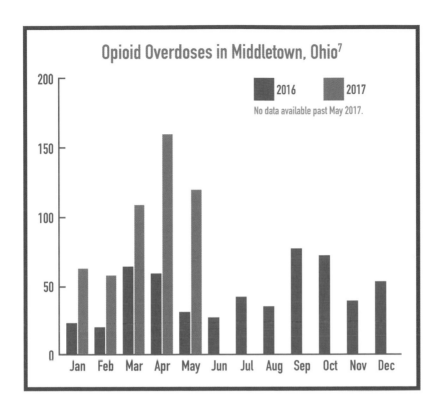

Opioid Overdoses in Middletown, Ohio[7]

■ 2016 ■ 2017

No data available past May 2017.

and both girls and boys are at high risk of developing sexually transmitted diseases.

Tragedies can result from addicted parents' habits and neglect. In 2015, 13-month-old Penny Cormani of Utah died after eating some of her parents' heroin. Both parents had been binging on heroin for several days and were too high to supervise their baby.

BABIES BORN ADDICTED

The number of babies born to mothers who use heroin and other opioids has also increased dramatically. Doctors advise pregnant

First Lady Melania Trump visited Lily's Place in 2017. This organization gives medical care to babies born with NAS.

women not to use any non-lifesaving drugs, but many addicted women continue to use while pregnant. Heroin and other opioids pass through the woman's placenta and into the fetus, and the baby becomes dependent on the drug. Before birth, opioid exposure can also lead to improper growth of the fetus and to premature birth. For instance, pregnant women who use heroin are more likely to experience a placental abruption, where the placenta tears away from the uterus, or other complications that make it necessary to deliver a baby before it is fully developed.

Studies on prescription opioid use during pregnancy indicate that some of these drugs, such as oxycodone and tramadol, are associated with an increased risk of preterm births. Other prescription opioids, including codeine and hydrocodone, do not seem to increase this risk. However, the risk of birth defects in newborns rises significantly when pregnant women use any of a variety of prescription opioids.

Babies exposed to heroin or prescription opioids before birth are usually born with neonatal abstinence syndrome (NAS). *Neonatal* refers to newborn babies. The word *abstinence* indicates that once these babies are born, the opioid they were getting from their mothers goes away, so they involuntarily abstain from receiving the drug. Studies indicate that the incidence of NAS has skyrocketed in recent years. In August 2016, the CDC reported the number of babies born addicted to opioids quadrupled between 1999 and 2013. West Virginia, Maine, Kentucky, Vermont, and New Mexico have been impacted especially severely. In West Virginia, approximately 33 of every 1,000 newborns were born with NAS in 2013.[8]

After they're born, NAS babies go through opioid

PREGNANT WOMEN AND OPIOIDS

Some states charge women who abuse opioids during pregnancy with child abuse. However, public health experts believe such penalties lead these women to avoid going to doctors. These experts therefore promote educating women about the dangers of using opioids while pregnant, and they advocate for enhancing access to contraception for at-risk women.

However, many women with addictions who are aware of the risks don't stop using drugs during pregnancy. Sheena was addicted to prescription opioids while pregnant. She said she could not quit, even knowing what might happen to her baby. "Just to get out of bed I had to have opiates. I was just in a place of complete self-hate," she explained.[9]

Some mothers who use drugs while pregnant feel guilty.

withdrawal. Symptoms usually start between 48 and 72 hours after birth. These symptoms include seizures, tremors, excessive and high-pitched screaming, irritability, yawning, a stuffy nose, vomiting, diarrhea, sleep problems, difficulties eating, dehydration, fever, sweating, and poor weight gain.

A 2016 study indicates that 86 percent of pregnancies among women who abuse opioids are unintentional.[11]

NAS babies stay in neonatal intensive care units in hospitals for an average of 23 days. They receive drugs such as morphine, methadone, or buprenorphine to diminish their withdrawal symptoms. Many NAS babies continue to grow poorly and may have ongoing seizures and other symptoms that require long-term treatment for opioid dependence.

The average hospital costs for treating a NAS infant total approximately $93,000. The yearly cost for such treatment in the United States is approximately $1.5 billion. Medicaid, the federal government program that pays for medical care for impoverished individuals, covers $1.2 billion of these costs.[10] Since American taxpayers pay for the consequences of pregnant women's opioid addictions, these expenditures have become a social issue. Many Americans have complained about the use of public funds to subsidize these addicted people's behaviors.

CHAPTER SIX

THE OPIOID EPIDEMIC

Studies indicate that rising rates of prescription opioid abuse are clearly linked to rising rates of heroin abuse and overdose deaths. In fact, 75 percent of new heroin users in the 2000s reported that they abused prescription opioids such as oxycodone before switching to heroin, according to a 2014 study by researchers at Washington University in St. Louis and Nova Southeastern University in Miami.[1] Furthermore, the CDC calls misuse of prescription opioids the strongest risk factor for starting to use heroin. It defines misuse as using more than a doctor prescribes, using the drugs with no medical need, or becoming addicted.

First responders across the country are being trained to use naloxone in the wake of the opioid epidemic.

NDC 69547-353-02

0.1 mL intranasal spray per unit
For use in the nose only

Rx Only

NARCAN®(naloxone HCl)
NASAL SPRAY 4 mg

Use NARCAN® Nasal Spray for known or suspected opioid overdose in adults and children.

Important: For use in the nose only.

Do not remove or test the NARCAN® Nasal Spray until ready to use.

This box contains **two (2)** 4-mg doses of naloxone HCl in 0.1 mL of nasal spray.

Two Pack

CHECK PRODUCT EXPIRATION DATE BEFORE USE.

OPEN HERE FOR QUICK START GUIDE
Opioid Overdose Response Instructions

Journalist Sam Quinones investigated and wrote about the forces underlying the opioid/heroin epidemic in his book *Dreamland*. He notes that the main forces were doctors' growing willingness to prescribe opioids for chronic pain; the development of pill mills, where

More than 276,000 adolescents aged 12 to 17 used prescription opioids for nonmedical reasons in 2015. Approximately 122,000 were addicted to these drugs.[2]

unscrupulous doctors prescribe unneeded opioids; and the introduction of black tar heroin by Mexican traffickers.

WILLINGNESS TO PRESCRIBE OPIOIDS

Until the late 1970s, most doctors thought opioids were too dangerous to prescribe for chronic pain or post-surgery pain. But then, research indicating that people in severe pain did not abuse opioids led to changes. Doctors prescribed more and more Vicodin, an opioid pain reliever, and similar pills for post-surgery and chronic pain patients. Many people kept using these pills after the need for them vanished. People discovered that they could crush and dissolve the pills to get high. Some people got hooked after a family member or friend gave them a sample. The United States rapidly became the world's largest consumer of opioid painkillers as doctors routinely prescribed these drugs for post-surgery or chronic pain patients. The number of prescriptions written for opioids quadrupled between 1999 and 2014. In 2014, millions of Americans reported that they had used prescription opioids for no medical purpose.

Many people abused OxyContin, which was introduced by the pharmaceutical company Purdue Pharma in 1996. The pill contains a special coating that makes it release its contents slowly over 12 hours. Purdue thought this would prevent abuse. As required by law, Purdue printed a warning label on pill bottles. The warning told consumers not to crush the pills because this could release "a potentially toxic amount of the drug."[3] But this warning let people know they could get high off the pills. Many people started crushing and snorting the contents to obtain 12 hours' worth of opioid effects.

Purdue sales representatives told doctors that only a small number of OxyContin users

OXYCONTIN AND THE HEROIN EPIDEMIC

In 2007, Purdue Pharma executives pleaded guilty to misbranding OxyContin. They admitted that they instructed their sales teams to tell doctors it was not addictive, while knowing it was. The guilty plea kept these individuals out of jail.

In 2010, Purdue released a new form of OxyContin that was more difficult to crush or dissolve. The company issued a statement noting that it did not know whether people would be able to abuse this new OxyContin. "There is no evidence that the reformulation of OxyContin is less subject to misuse, abuse, diversion, overdose or addiction," the statement read.[4] It turned out people could not abuse the new version, but those addicted to OxyContin switched to heroin. This had unintended effects. According to a January 2017 report by researchers at the National Bureau of Economic Research, "a substantial share of the dramatic increase in heroin deaths since 2010 can be attributed to the reformulation of OxyContin."[5]

became addicted. Doctors began prescribing large amounts of the drug. Many patients who became addicted started doctor shopping—visiting numerous doctors' offices to obtain identical prescriptions for pills to satisfy their cravings.

PILL MILLS

As more and more Americans used opioids in the late 1990s, numerous doctors opened so-called pill mills. These were medical clinics that supposedly served people with chronic pain. Many doctors who ran pill mills had previous medical license violations. Some were convicted felons. These physicians rarely required their patients to provide proof of a painful condition. They dispensed prescriptions to anyone willing to pay cash for a monthly appointment.

Many patients who shopped for doctors received hundreds of pills per month from pill mills. Medical insurance plans or the government's Medicaid program paid for many of these pills. Many people with addictions sold their extra pills illegally at a huge profit. Street drug dealers started selling OxyContin and other opioids as well.

Most adolescents who abuse prescription pain relievers report that they initially obtained the drugs for free from a family member or friend.

Pill mills led to increased deaths from opioid overdoses. Drug rehabilitation clinics started seeing large numbers of people addicted to opioids who wanted to quit. Illegal sales of prescription opioids made prices rise. Illegally obtained OxyContin often costs one dollar per milligram (0.001 g). For example, a 40-milligram (0.04 g) pill costs $40.[6] Many people with addictions couldn't afford these prices. The US government also started shutting down pill mills during the 2000s. This made it more difficult for people with addictions to obtain the pills.

PILL MILLS FUELED ADDICTION

Many addiction experts believe the main factor that drove the opioid epidemic that began in the late 1990s was pill mills. Ed Hughes ran an addiction counseling clinic in Portsmouth, Ohio. He stated that addiction spread "like a wildfire" once pill mills became prevalent in the area. Long lines of patients waited for opioid prescriptions every day at pill mills. The book *Dreamland* says a pill mill is "a virtual ATM for dope."[8]

EXPLOITING THE OPIOID CRISIS

At the same time, Mexican heroin dealers and other drug traffickers "exploited America's prescription opioid addiction, flooding the market with heroin, a cheaper and more readily available alternative," according to the Drug Enforcement Agency (DEA). Drug traffickers make huge profits from selling heroin. They can earn several hundred thousand dollars by selling 2.2 pounds (1 kg) of the drug.[7] Farmers in the Xalisco area of Mexico formerly grew sugarcane, but many switched to opium poppies in the 1990s after realizing how profitable they

In 2012, police in Minnesota confiscated black tar heroin found in a hotel.

were. The huge heroin market in the United States led opium production in Mexico to increase drastically in 2014.

Mexican dealers from Xalisco began smuggling and selling pure, high-quality black tar heroin in the western United States in the 1990s. Soon, this type of heroin spread nationwide. The dealers continue to operate differently than most drug cartels. Independent dealers set up call centers to take calls from people who want heroin delivered. Drivers then deliver the heroin at prearranged places. The convenience of delivery and the purity of black tar heroin led to increasing numbers of loyal customers. Narcotics officer Dennis Chavez at the Denver Police Department was one of the first to investigate these independent dealers. He started calling them the Xalisco Boys.

The plentiful supply and relatively inexpensive price of black tar heroin led the number of addicted people to grow steadily in the 2000s. The typical price for white powder heroin from drug cartels is approximately $100 for a bag of weak, diluted heroin that satisfies an addicted person for half a day. In contrast, the cost is approximately $40 for pure, black tar heroin that creates a high that lasts a full day. In 2007, 373,000 Americans reported that they used heroin. In 2011, this number had grown to 620,000.[9] In 2014, it was 914,000.[10]

THE XALISCO BOYS

The Xalisco Boys operate independent heroin dealerships across the United States. The people who deliver heroin carry the drug in their mouths in 15 to 25 uninflated balloons. They hide another 100 balloons in their cars.[11] If police stop and arrest them, they swallow the balloons in their mouths. Most who are caught with small amounts of heroin are deported, but new drivers immediately replace them.

NEW REGULATIONS

New government regulations also worsened the heroin epidemic. In 2014 and 2016, the CDC issued guidelines for doctors who prescribe opioids. These guidelines recommended prescribing opioids for shorter durations and in lower doses, regardless of patients' individual needs. The CDC and DEA also began to closely monitor these doctors. They took away the medical licenses of some who did not comply with these guidelines. Many frightened doctors started dramatically reducing patients' dosages. Many stopped prescribing opioids, even to people in horrific pain.

Desperate patients started buying opioid pills on the street. When this became too expensive, many switched to heroin. Some patients won't risk buying illegal drugs and have become bedridden because of their pain. Others have committed suicide because the pain got so bad. Many doctors are concerned about how government regulations are affecting people with a genuine need for powerful painkillers. Many are also concerned that the regulations are feeding the heroin overdose death epidemic.

ATHLETES AND OPIOIDS

Athletes are widely affected by doctors' willingness to prescribe opioid pain medications. In one survey, more than 1,000 former National Football League players claimed their teams freely gave opioids to injured players so they could keep playing.[12] Many players became addicted.

High school athletes also report widespread opioid use. For example, coaches gave Vicodin to a soccer player named Amy for a sprained ankle. She began taking higher and higher doses to get high. She bought the pills illegally after doctors stopped prescribing them. When this became too expensive, she tried black tar heroin. Amy died after injecting her first dose.

STIGMA AND DRUG ABUSE

Heroin and prescription opioid use are associated with significant stigma. According to public health expert Lauren Villa, "Stigma results in prejudice, avoidance, rejection and discrimination against people who have a socially undesirable trait or engage in culturally marginalized behaviors, such as drug abuse."[1] The stigma that surrounds drug abuse and addiction shapes public policies. It also affects the self-esteem and lives of people with addictions and their families. Stigma has affected people with addictions for decades.

By 1900, approximately 300,000 people in the United States were addicted to heroin. Approximately two-thirds were

The war on drugs has sent many people to prison for drug-related crimes.

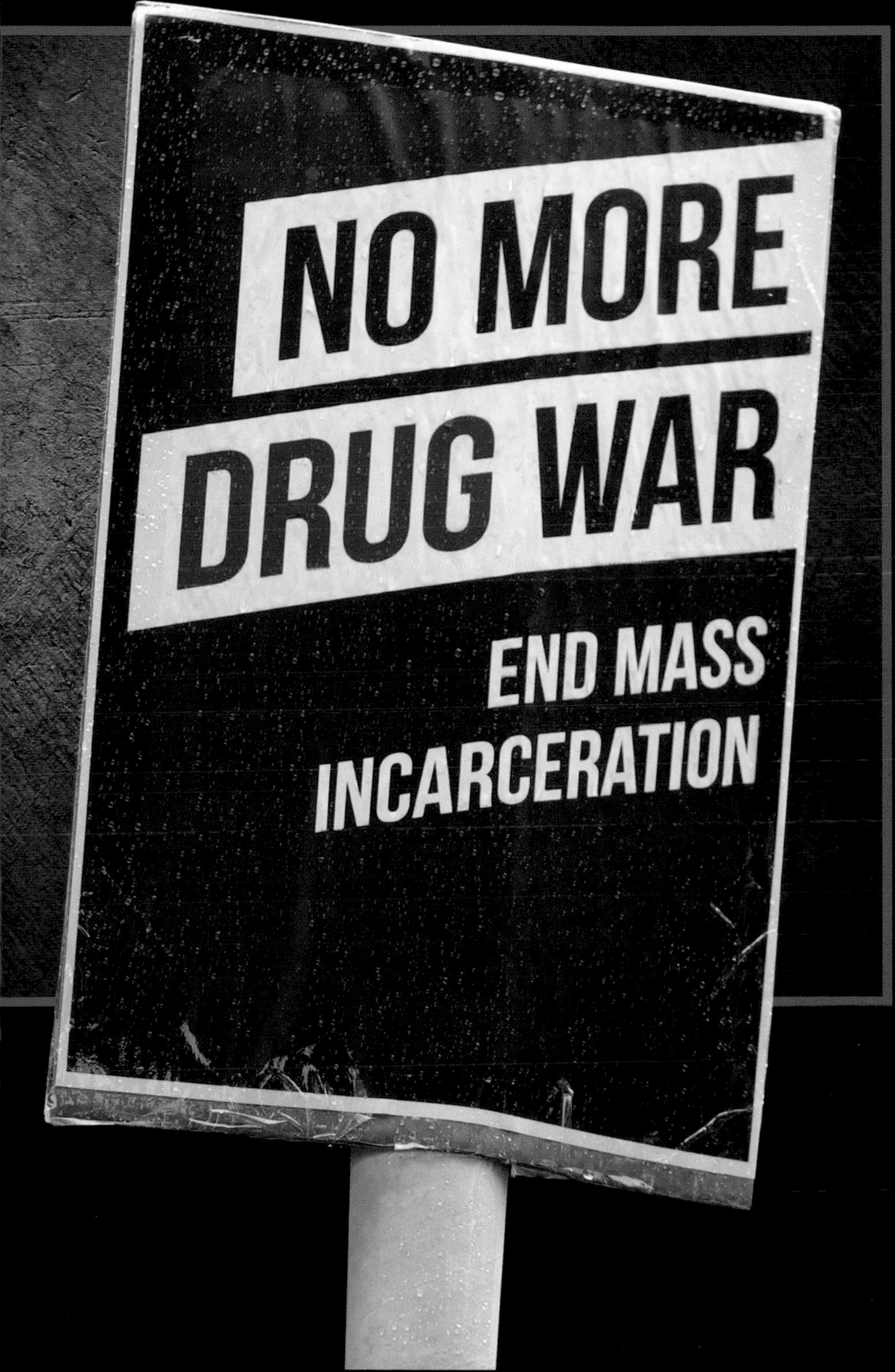
NO MORE
DRUG WAR
END MASS
INCARCERATION

middle- and upper-class women who used heroin to alleviate medical ailments.[2] Others generally regarded them with pity, but in the 1910s and 1920s, attitudes about heroin and addiction changed.

In 1914, Congress passed the Harrison Narcotics Tax Act, in part to discourage addicted people from stealing money to finance their heroin habit. The law imposed a tax on heroin. It also allowed doctors to prescribe the drug, but not to people with addictions. People with addictions started buying heroin illegally from drug traffickers. In addition, heroin use became prevalent in slums, where many recently arrived immigrants lived. Many people with addictions joined gangs and became drug dealers to finance their habit. According to history professor David T. Courtwright, society began to associate heroin addiction with unsavory people. Addiction evolved "from being a pathetic condition to a stigmatized one. Like venereal disease, it came to be understood as something that was acquired through forbidden indulgence with evil associates."[3]

In the mid-1920s, the government launched a campaign to shame what it called "dope fiends." It labeled people with addictions as "deviant, crime-prone, weak-willed moral failures."[4] The government also updated the 1914 Harrison Narcotics Tax Act in 1924 and made heroin illegal. This contributed greatly to the associated stigma.

The "Just Say No" campaign created by First Lady Nancy Reagan in the 1980s was ineffective, but it made an attempt at combating the drug problem in the United States.

Dr. Nora Volkow notes that the stigma associated with addiction has far-reaching effects on public policy and even on scientific research. "For much of the past century, scientists studying drug abuse labored in the shadow of powerful myths and misconceptions about the nature of addiction," she states. "When scientists began to study addictive behavior in the 1930s, people addicted to drugs were thought to be morally flawed and lacking in willpower. Those views shaped society's responses to drug abuse, treating it as a moral failing rather than as a health problem, which led to an emphasis on punishment rather than prevention and treatment."[5]

STIGMA IN THE 2000s

Today, government agencies and addiction experts are more likely to view addiction as a disease than as a moral flaw. Many

THE JOHNS HOPKINS STUDY

A 2014 study by researchers at the Johns Hopkins Bloomberg School of Public Health in Maryland found that the stigma attached to drug addiction is far more intense and pervasive than that attached to mental illness. For example, 90 percent of Americans are unwilling to have someone who is addicted to drugs marry into their family. Fifty-nine percent feel this way about people with mental illness. Seventy-eight percent are unwilling to work closely with a person who is addicted to drugs compared to 38 percent for someone with mental illness.

Other findings were that 63 percent of the survey respondents think discrimination against people with addictions is "not a serious problem." Sixty-four percent said it's fine for employers to not hire someone with a drug addiction. Fifty-four percent said landlords should be allowed to deny housing to people with drug addictions.[8]

people who support the disease theory thought it would lessen the stigma by removing the personal blame argument. However, addiction-related stigma and shame are still prevalent. As addiction expert Dr. Akikur Mohammad states in his book *The Anatomy of Addiction*, "Public opinion about addiction has not yet caught up with the science."[6] Indeed, the President's Commission on Combating Drug Addiction and the Opioid Crisis and other US government groups report that shame and stigma keep most people with addictions from seeking help. Only 10 percent of these people receive treatment.[7] Conversely, people who do not feel stigmatized or judged are more willing to seek treatment and recovery, according to lawyer Marie Borland, who serves as president of Changing Minds Tampa.

However, hysteria over the opioid epidemic has also stigmatized chronic pain patients who responsibly take prescription opioids and do not have addictions to opioids. Edwina Caito takes prescription opioids as prescribed by her doctor to help her function with horrific pain from fibromyalgia. "I feel this stigma every single day: You're a chronic pain patient, you must be an addict," she states.[9] Cato notes that harsh government regulations adopted to control the opioid epidemic disregard the fact that many people with chronic pain need and benefit from these drugs.

Shame also causes many people with addictions to avoid social situations. Villa explains that when people feel stigmatized, they "feel pushed to the outskirts of society and may lose touch with their community and family and experience profound loneliness and isolation."[10] This alienation

IMPACTS ON CHILDREN

Journalist David Sheff has written extensively about drug addiction. He notes that children whose parents are addicted to drugs often feel shame and loneliness because of the way society stigmatizes addiction. "If a parent had a heart problem or cancer or something like that, it'd be talked about in school with teachers, there would be support, other families would be offering to help with childcare, bringing casseroles over," Sheff states. "But with this problem, because it is perceived to be a problem of choice and morals, the child is shamed. There's no sense of community support and so they're further isolated."[11]

often leads people with addictions to increase their drug use to dull their feelings of rejection.

MEDICAL STIGMA

In some cases, the attitude of health-care professionals reflects the stigma associated with drug addiction. Many doctors will not treat people with addictions in their medical offices. Some refuse because they view addiction treatment as futile. Most people with addictions end up relapsing multiple times, and these physicians think treatment is useless because recovery is not usually permanent.

Labels such as *junkie* help perpetuate the stigma associated with heroin addiction.

Some medical professionals who have internalized the cultural bias against drug users even shame sober patients. Tracey Helton Mitchell had used heroin, but she had been sober for years before she found that many nurses held preconceived ideas about people with addictions. Mitchell achieved a lasting recovery long before she started having children. After her first baby was born, she breastfed the newborn in her hospital bed. Several nurses asked her, "Are you sure you should be breastfeeding the baby with your history?" After one such comment, Mitchell recalled that she "wanted to throw something across the room." Then, she wondered why this nurse could not "see that I'm a new person."[12] Mitchell realized that because of the stigma that plagues drug users, her history with drug abuse would always remain a part of her.

MULTIPLE STIGMATIZED DISEASES

Another factor that enhances stigma is that many drug abusers also have mental illnesses such as schizophrenia or bipolar disorder. Many also develop infectious diseases such as hepatitis C or HIV through sharing needles or having unprotected sex. Drug addiction, mental illness, and sexually transmitted infections are among the most-stigmatized diseases in the world. Having a combination of these diseases magnifies the stigma and shame associated with each. Therefore, affected individuals are unlikely to seek treatment. But without treatment, they are more likely to pass the transmittable diseases to others.

Yet, experts stress that people with all these ailments need the most help. Those who do seek help are shown to benefit from medical and psychological treatments for each illness. For example, studies indicate that combining

DANGERS OF STIGMA

Claire Foster was addicted to heroin but stopped using it. Yet she hesitates to tell others about her past. That's because the usual reaction is "a blank, panicked stare." Foster thinks other peoples' "ignorance and fear is a much greater risk to me than a relapse. . . . If I am honest about my addiction, I could lose my job, my home, and custody of my child. I could be denied medical care."[13] So she asks society to help banish stigma by looking beyond the label and at the person she has become.

Treatment programs give people with addictions the opportunity to find support.

drug abuse counseling with HIV prevention education reduces heroin use and risky behaviors such as sharing needles. The main challenge is motivating people to stay in treatment and follow-up programs.

SHAMING VERSUS HELPING

Experts and people impacted by the opioid epidemic believe enhancing public awareness is critical for diminishing stigma. However, some believe that publicity intended to raise awareness can shame people with addictions and therefore ends up being a negative influence. For example, in 2016, Ohio police released a photo of 47-year-old James Lee Accord and 50-year-old Rhonda L. Pasek passed out from a heroin overdose in the front seat of their car. Their four-year-old son sat in the back seat. This photo was widely shared on social media and became a symbol of the opioid epidemic. Some praised police for putting faces on those impacted by the epidemic. But others, such as *Vox* journalist German Lopez, criticized the publicity: "Shaming the parents, as many were quick to do on social media, won't help them break their drug addiction. Getting them—and other drug users—medical care and treatment for a drug abuse disorder will."[14]

When opioid and heroin overdoses began killing more and more people around the year 2000, shame led most families to keep quiet about what killed their loved ones. But around 2009, numerous parents of young people who died began speaking out to warn other families of the risks. They decided that educating the public would allow some good to come from their personal tragedies. Some founded grief-support organizations; others spoke out individually. Many also began educating lawmakers and public health officials about the epidemic.

THE DISEASE MODEL AND STIGMA

Those who believe addiction is a disease also believe this view diminishes stigma. However, a 2014 study in Australia found that calling addiction a disease has not affected stigma. It has also not diminished support for punishing people who have addictions.

In addition, a 2014 study at the University of British Columbia found that calling addiction a disease increased feelings of shame in people with an addiction to alcohol. It decreased their belief that they could control their behavior. Psychiatrist Joan Trujols concludes, "So far, the claim that framing addiction as a brain disease will lead to stigma reduction seems to be an unrealistically rosy picture."[15]

PREVENTION AND TREATMENT

Lawmakers, public health agencies, and individuals are taking steps to control the opioid/heroin epidemic through prevention and treatment programs. One method of preventing drug abuse is school-based education programs. The Drug Abuse Resistance Education (D.A.R.E.) program was introduced in 1983 for this purpose. However, most authorities believe D.A.R.E. was largely ineffective because it lectured kids rather than involving them in interactive activities. Experts at universities and government agencies therefore put together a new program called Keepin' it REAL in 2009. Studies indicate this

People can receive naloxone overdose kits to help prevent overdose deaths.

program has reduced drug abuse and fostered antidrug attitudes among children and teenagers. The program engages middle school kids in role-playing with their peers. These activities help them develop effective decision-making strategies, which spell out the REAL acronym: Refuse, Explain, Avoid, Leave.

Another effective method of educating and influencing young people is having individuals recovering from addictions tell young people their stories. Many people who overcome addiction become addiction counselors or public speakers for this purpose. Chris Herren speaks regularly to students. After losing his basketball career and suffering four near-fatal overdoses within eight years, Herren entered rehab and got clean at age 32. Herren emphasizes the importance of talking to counselors about issues before things progress to the point of using drugs to cope. School officials and others call his talks inspiring. Many students cry during his presentations and talk with counselors afterward.

One reason preventing addiction is so important is that many addicted people become disabled and cannot function. In fact, the Substance Abuse and Mental Health Services Administration predicts that "by 2020 mental and substance use disorders will surpass all physical diseases as a major cause of disability worldwide."[1]

COMPREHENSIVE TREATMENT

While drug abuse prevention is more desirable than treatment, improving treatment for people with addictions is also important. Experts believe that increasing access to comprehensive treatment programs is critical for solving the opioid crisis. The US government is expanding this access under the Affordable Care Act. Comprehensive treatment includes Medication-Assisted Treatment (MAT), which incorporates medicines that help addicted people get through withdrawal and other medications that reduce drug cravings; psychotherapy; and support programs. The combination of these different treatment types has proven to reduce overdose deaths, relapses, transmission of infectious diseases, and criminal activity in people with addictions. It benefits individuals, families, and society.

There are more addiction rehabilitation clinics in the United States than there are Starbucks coffee shops.

However, Dr. Akikur Mohammad notes that in 2015, 90 percent of the 14,000 drug rehabilitation clinics in the United States did not use proven medical treatments.[2] He believes these clinics avoid what he calls "evidence-based medicine" because it would reduce their profits. "It would greatly increase the cost of doing business and diminish profits if rehab clinics adopted a scientific approach to treating addiction," he writes in his book *The Anatomy of Addiction*.[3]

A study by CASA found that most addiction counselors at rehab clinics and 12-step programs are underqualified. "Most of those providing addiction care are not medical professionals

LESSONS FROM VIETNAM

In 1971, Congressmen Robert Steele and Morgan Murphy visited American soldiers who were fighting in the Vietnam War (1954–1975). They discovered that approximately 15 percent were addicted to heroin.[5] The drug was cheap and widely available in Vietnam. President Richard Nixon promised to help these soldiers overcome their addictions. He commissioned psychiatric researcher Lee Robins and her colleagues to study the soldiers' progress.

Robins found that 95 percent of the soldiers overcame their addictions and did not relapse after returning to the United States. This was puzzling, since previous research indicated that 90 percent of people addicted to heroin relapsed after recovering.[6] More research determined the change in environment helped the addicted people. This is because habits that are repeated in the same setting become tied to that setting. Changing the environment frees these behaviors from being automatically repeated. Some psychologists therefore encourage people with addictions to change aspects of their environment to aid in recovery.

and are not equipped with the knowledge, skills, or credentials necessary to provide the full range of effective treatments," the study states.[4] Medical authorities hope more clinics will incorporate MAT to give addicted people the best chance for long-term recovery. Even then, most people with addictions end up relapsing at some point because of the power of addiction.

STARTING TREATMENT

The first step in any treatment program is for the addicted person to decide if he or she truly wants to stop his or her addiction. After this decision, the next step is detoxification. Here, the addicted person receives medicine to help with withdrawal.

After detoxification, ongoing treatment with medications that block cravings for heroin or prescription opioids is sometimes recommended. These medications act on the same opioid receptors that opioid drugs do. However, they are less addictive. People on these drugs are less likely to engage in compulsive drug-seeking behaviors. The specific drugs used depend on individual needs.

One category of maintenance drug is opioid agonists. These drugs activate opioid receptors like heroin and prescription opioids do. Another category is partial opioid agonists. They activate opioid receptors much less than opioid drugs do. A third category is opioid antagonists. They block opioid receptors so the users cannot feel the pleasurable effects if they take heroin or prescription opioids.

Methadone is a widely used opioid agonist that reaches the brain slowly. It prevents euphoria and withdrawal and has positive long-term effects in some people. Studies indicate that methadone is effective in 60 to 90 percent of people with addictions who use it consistently.[7] However, methadone users can overdose. Many patients also resent having to come to a treatment clinic every day to receive methadone. This is why many treatment centers have switched to using buprenorphine.

Buprenorphine is a partial opioid agonist. It reduces cravings for opioids but does not produce euphoria. It also does not affect breathing, so it can reduce overdose deaths. Suboxone is one commonly used form of buprenorphine. It also contains the opioid antagonist naloxone. This helps it block the feelings of euphoria people with addictions might feel if they ingest heroin or other opioids.

Doctors, nurse practitioners, and physician assistants must be certified to prescribe Suboxone. Many experts believe Suboxone or plain buprenorphine should be used more often because they're safer than methadone. They're also effective pain relievers. Some suggest these drugs could be used instead of addictive prescription opioids. Dr. Joseph Mancini calls buprenorphine "the only safe opioid."[8]

PSYCHOLOGICAL TREATMENT AND SUPPORT PROGRAMS

Psychological counseling is another important component

HEROIN AND PRESCRIPTION OPIOID VACCINES

A potential method of preventing or treating opioid addiction is with vaccines. Vaccines are drugs that prevent illness by stimulating the immune system to create antibodies, or chemicals that fight off specific foreign substances. Some vaccines block the effects of an addictive drug. Scientists at The Scripps Research Institute (TSRI) in La Jolla, California, are testing vaccines that block the effects of heroin and prescription opioids.

The scientists created a heroin vaccine that causes the immune system to neutralize heroin's effects before the drug reaches the brain. This prevents users from getting high. The vaccine works well in laboratory rats and rhesus monkeys. The researchers plan to test it on humans. They also created another vaccine that neutralizes and prevents overdoses of oxycodone and hydrocodone. So far, it works well in mice.

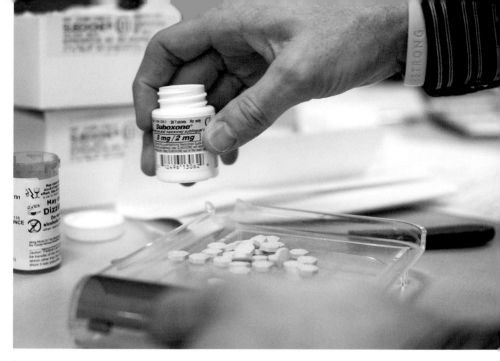

Suboxone eliminates cravings and withdrawal.

of opioid addiction treatment. Studies indicate that the combination of medications, psychotherapy, and support programs is more effective than any treatment type used alone. Most therapists employ variations of cognitive behavioral therapy or contingency management therapy. Cognitive behavioral therapy involves the therapist helping the addicted person think differently about himself or herself. This helps the individual control responses to stress and subsequent behaviors. For example, rather than coping with an emotion or difficult situation by taking opioids, the individual might learn to speak with a friend or practice meditation.

In contingency management therapy, patients are rewarded for practicing healthy habits. For instance, testing negative for illegal drugs might allow the individual to earn points that can be exchanged for something like a nice dinner in a restaurant.

Twelve-step or similar programs such as Narcotics Anonymous also aid recovery, especially when combined with psychotherapy and MAT. Dr. Drew Pinsky notes that one advantage of 12-step programs is that they provide human connections. As Pinsky writes, "Every one of my patients enjoying successful recovery has discovered that the only way to get past pain, fear, and feelings of powerlessness or insignificance is by connecting with other people. They do it in meetings, with sponsors, with family and friends. These new relationships are the building blocks of a new life."[9]

Twelve-step programs such as those offered by Narcotics Anonymous involve members regularly attending meetings with other people recovering from addictions. These individuals share stories about the challenges and triumphs

ACHIEVING SOBRIETY

Many addiction counselors and people with addictions view staying away from heroin or prescription opioids as the hallmark of recovery. However, neuroscientist Marc Lewis believes the focus on recovery stems from the erroneous view that addiction is a disease. People seek to recover, or go back to the way they were before getting sick, from diseases. But Lewis points out that many formerly addicted people who achieve lasting sobriety view this transformation as moving forward to become a stronger person. "Instead of recovering, it seems that addicts keep growing, as does anyone who overcomes their difficulties through deliberation and insight," he writes.[10]

Narcotics Anonymous meetings give addicted people the chance to talk about their addiction.

in their journey to overcome narcotic addictions. Members in recovery often sponsor others trying to attain sobriety and serve as supportive mentors. These programs require addicted people to completely abstain from drug use. This is because their guiding philosophy is that people with addictions are powerless to stop abusing drugs unless they resist taking that first dose.

LAWS AND POLICIES

In August 2017, President Donald Trump declared the opioid crisis a "public health emergency."[1] The release of a preliminary report by the President's Commission on Combating Drug Addiction and the Opioid Crisis followed Trump's announcement. This report calls the epidemic unprecedented and compares its impact to that of the terrorist attacks of September 11, 2001: "America is enduring a death toll equal to September 11 every three weeks."[2] The commission notes that Trump's declaration of a public health emergency will expedite funding for solutions to the opioid crisis. It also allows government departments to act quickly to implement new laws and regulations as needed.

In some drug abuse prevention programs, police officers are invited into classrooms to discuss the impacts of drugs.

The government has recruited a variety of medical, legal, and policy experts to address the heroin/opioid crisis. However, the complex causes and issues of addiction make it difficult to develop and implement solutions.

THE WAR ON DRUGS

One reason it's difficult to change existing drug policies and laws is that the so-called war on drugs has shaped US policy since the 1970s. In 1971, President Richard Nixon declared the war on drugs, which mainly sought to lock up and punish people with addictions for corrupting society. One element of this war involved increasing the size and reach of government drug-control agencies. Another was passing laws that imposed mandatory jail sentences for possession and use of illegal drugs.

Enforcement of these antidrug laws vastly increased the prison population nationwide. The government has spent approximately $51 billion

UNDERREPORTING OVERDOSE DEATHS

A 2017 study by public policy expert Christopher J. Ruhm at the University of Virginia revealed that one-fifth to one-fourth of deaths from heroin and other opioid overdoses are reported inaccurately. Ruhm found that this happens because many medical examiners who prepare death certificates do not name the drug responsible for the death. He believes inaccurate information of this type is a "barrier to formulating effective policies to address the rapid rise in U.S. fatal overdoses."[4] Ruhm therefore encourages medical examiners to list the precise cause of death to help with policy decisions.

per year fighting this war since 1971.[3] Yet it has not reduced the prevalence or consequences of drug addiction. The consensus

among policy experts is that the war on drugs has failed. Most medical authorities and policymakers now believe the focus should shift to helping people who are addicted to drugs, rather than locking them up. Studies also show that it's much cheaper to treat drug addictions than it is to incarcerate people with addictions.

One type of service that many communities are implementing to help addicted people is needle exchange programs, also known as syringe services programs. These programs provide free syringes for injection-drug users at clinics or selected pharmacies. Not reusing syringes is proven to reduce the spread of infectious diseases like AIDS and hepatitis among addicted people. In 2016, Congress passed the Consolidated Appropriations Act. This legislation provides federal funds for states and localities that want to start needle exchange programs that conform to rules laid out by the CDC.

LEGAL SOLUTIONS

One trend that has expanded in recent years is drug courts. Drug courts give people with addictions the opportunity to avoid going to jail if they agree to enter a treatment plan. In a

INCREASING ACCESS TO NALOXONE

Hospital emergency rooms have used naloxone for many years to reverse the effects of opioid overdoses. In recent years, public health agencies have promoted policies that allow people who may come in contact with overdoses to carry naloxone. One recommendation these agencies make is that all emergency responders should carry it. In April 2017, New Mexico was the first state to require police officers to carry naloxone. Other agencies have proposed that teachers, parents, coaches, and employers should be trained to watch for signs of overdose and to administer naloxone.

drug court, a team consisting of a judge, prosecutor, defense attorney, treatment provider, probation officer, and other professionals keeps track of a drug abuser's progress in a treatment program. The user is subject to frequent drug tests and must also attend drug counseling sessions. Drug courts have proved to help people with addictions stay sober and to reduce drug-associated crimes.

Another policy shift occurred when Congress passed the Comprehensive Addiction and Recovery Act of 2016 to reduce penalties for minor drug crimes. Possession of small amounts of heroin is now considered a minor drug crime. As such, federal law mandates a minimum sentence of no more than one year in prison, a minimum fine of $1,000, or both.[5] Before, people could spend years in prison. This legislation also expanded access to treatment programs and to the drug naloxone to help save lives when people experience an opioid overdose. In addition, it highlighted new guidelines for prescribing opioid painkillers and outlined ways in which communities can address prescription opioid abuse.

State laws are also changing policy approaches to opioid addictions. For example, in July 2017, the Oregon legislature passed a law that reduced jail time and fines for nonviolent first-time offenders caught with small amounts of heroin or other illegal drugs. It reclassifies possession of small amounts of these drugs as a misdemeanor instead of a felony. Other states, including California, Colorado, Delaware, Iowa, Massachusetts, Pennsylvania, and New York, have enacted similar laws.

Many states have also passed new laws regulating prescription opioids. For instance, in 2017, New Jersey passed a law that requires prescribers to document their attempts to treat chronic pain without prescription opioids before they prescribe these drugs. The law also requires prescribers to carefully monitor patients who take prescription opioids. In

PORTUGAL DECRIMINALIZES DRUG ABUSE

In 2000, Portugal decriminalized possession of all drugs, including heroin. Instead of being jailed, users are ordered to begin treatment programs. However, drug dealers and traffickers who sell drugs on the street are still sent to jail.

Since then, rates of people with addictions spreading infectious diseases have declined. Overdose deaths are also less common. Portuguese government policy expert and physician João Goulão believes the positive results stem from viewing addiction as a chronic health issue rather than as a crime. "It was really important for our society because it allowed us to drop the stigma," he stated.[6]

addition, new prescriptions for opioid painkillers can include only a five-day supply.

PENALTIES FOR TRAFFICKERS

Penalties for drug dealers or traffickers are much more severe than those for drug users. These offenses usually result in felonies. Legal experts often refer to these crimes as "possession with the intent to distribute."[7] But all aspects of manufacturing, transporting, and selling illegal drugs fall under laws that regulate drug trafficking.

The severity of trafficking penalties usually depends on the particular state in which the crime occurred. But some traffickers are prosecuted by the federal government. This is likely to happen if crimes occurred in multiple states. The severity of trafficking penalties also depends on the amount of opioids sold and the number of previous offenses the criminal has. For example, someone charged with his or her second federal drug offense who is caught with 200 grams (0.2 kg) of heroin faces 20 years to life in prison and a fine of up to $20 million.[8]

In some states, such as Pennsylvania, heroin users and sellers can be charged with separate crimes for possessing heroin paraphernalia such as syringes, spoons, or lighters used for smoking the drug.

Laws passed since 2012 make it easier to increase penalties for traffickers who use a weapon or are leaders in trafficking organizations. In 2016, approximately 96 percent of the drug traffickers caught were sent to prison. The average prison term was 63 months.[9]

Penalties for drug trafficking offenders prosecuted by states also depend on the amount of heroin and the number of previous offenses. For instance, in Texas, possessing one to four grams (0.001 to 0.004 kg) of heroin is a second-degree felony. Penalties can range from 2 to 20 years in jail and up to a $10,000 fine. Possession of 200 to 400 grams (0.2 to 0.4 kg) is a first-degree felony. It is punishable with 10 to 99 years in jail and up to a $100,000 fine.[10]

Federal and state laws also dictate mandatory minimum sentences for drug offenders. For example, under federal law, anyone who participates in a drug deal near a school or who intentionally sells drugs to someone under 21 is subject to a minimum sentence of twice the usual minimum.

Rules for imposing twice the minimum penalties also apply to people (other than licensed pharmacists) who sell prescription

EDUCATE AND HELP, NOT PUNISH

California judge James Gray writes in his book *Why Our Drug Laws Have Failed and What We Can Do About It* that instead of focusing on punishing people with addictions, he believes a focus on widespread education and help for people with addictions would be more productive: "We have never been a drug-free society and we never will be. Recognizing this fact. . . we should try to employ an approach that will most effectively reduce the deaths, disease, crime, and misery caused by their presence in our communities."[11]

Many first responders are trained in providing assistance to individuals experiencing an opioid overdose.

opioids. It is also illegal under federal and state laws to use these drugs recreationally, to possess them without a valid doctor's prescription, or to share them with anyone. Simply possessing prescription opioids without a prescription can lead to penalties of 1 to 5 years in prison plus fines, depending on state laws. Penalties for possessing with intent to sell can result in 5 to 20 years in prison, fines of $250,000 to $5 million, or both.[12]

OTHER NEW LAWS

Policy experts are also promoting new laws that remove penalties for people who help overdose victims. Many people

hesitate to help or to even call for help. Families of overdose victims have sued people for helping if something goes wrong, such as the overdose victim dying despite efforts to save him or her. As of July 2017, 40 US states and the District of Columbia had passed so-called Good Samaritan or 911 immunity laws and were striving to educate the public about these laws.

Other policy changes focus on curbing shopping for doctors and closing down pill mills. It's difficult for officials to police doctor shopping because people who obtain multiple prescriptions from numerous doctors rarely use medical insurance to pay for the drugs. But several US states have implemented computerized monitoring systems that track opioid prescriptions filled at certain pharmacies. It is as yet unknown whether these efforts will pay off.

In approximately 2010, DEA agents began investigating, raiding, and shutting down pill mills. Many pill mill doctors went to jail and lost their medical licenses. Places such as Florida that were heavily impacted by pill mills also passed laws that limited the number of opioid pills patients could receive each month. Doctors who legitimately prescribe opioids are required to check a statewide database to find out whether their patients have been caught or convicted of doctor shopping or drug dealing.

A SLOW PROCESS

Complex personal and social factors mean that controlling the opioid/heroin epidemic will take time. "No one thinks the recovery from this is going to be fast," states Caleb Alexander of the Johns Hopkins Center for Drug Safety and Effectiveness.[13] This is partly because deeply entrenched cultural trends must be addressed.

After studying the epidemic for several years while writing his book *Dreamland*, Sam Quinones notes that many Americans turn to drugs for comfort because society's basic values have deteriorated. "Heroin is, I believe, the final expression of values we have fostered for thirty-five years. It turns every addict into narcissistic, self-absorbed, solitary hyper-consumers," he writes.[14] Quinones partly blames the American obsession with technology for these values. A large majority of children watch television and play computer games instead of playing outdoors like their grandparents did. Family members interact through text messages. This isolates children and teaches them that technology, rather than interpersonal interactions, are important. Some of these kids thus never learn to turn to loved ones for support or comfort when adversity strikes. But whatever factors are driving the epidemic, Quinones and others hope that increased awareness about it will be a force for positive change.

In 2017, lawmakers studied ways to handle the opioid crisis at the President's Commission on Combating Drug Addiction and the Opioid Crisis.

ESSENTIAL FACTS

EFFECTS ON THE BODY

- The number one cause of accidental deaths in the United States is drug overdoses. In 2017, more than 140 Americans died every day from a drug overdose.

- Opioid users experience a variety of short-term effects such as euphoria, pain relief, drowsiness, slowed breathing and heart rate, nausea, vomiting, constricted pupils, dry mouth, flushing of the skin, and a heavy feeling in the arms and legs.

- Long-term opioid users experience a variety of physical and psychological problems including heart and liver disease, insomnia, constipation, and lung diseases such as pneumonia and tuberculosis.

LAWS AND POLICIES

- Heroin is an illegal substance in the United States.

- Prescription opioids are legal, but people need a doctor's prescription in order to purchase them. Legal prescription opioids include morphine, fentanyl, oxycodone, and hydrocodone.

- Naloxone can be used on people experiencing an opioid overdose. It's used to reverse the effects of an overdose. Many lawmakers and public health officials are trying to expand people's access to naloxone.

- Most policymakers and medical authorities think the focus of laws and public policies should shift from punishing people with drug addictions to helping them.

- A variety of medical, legal, and policy experts have been recruited by the government to address the heroin/opioid crisis. But the complex issues make it difficult to create solutions.

- Using vaccines is a potential method of preventing or treating heroin and prescription opioid addiction.

- The goal of addiction treatment is to help the individual achieve the longest possible recovery periods by making follow-up medical and behavioral tools accessible.

- Learning new methods of coping with life plays a central role in helping people recovering from addiction achieve lasting sobriety.

IMPACT ON SOCIETY

- Communities such as Middletown, Ohio, are plagued by the opioid epidemic. Crime rates and the expense of paying first responders to aid people experiencing overdoses have increased.

- Many families have been impacted by the opioid epidemic. Children have overdosed and died after using heroin or prescription opioids.

- Heroin and prescription opioid abusers today can be virtually anyone, including suburban housewives, grandparents, families in rural areas, and middle- or upper-class students.

- The stigma attached to drug addiction is more intense than the stigma attached to mental illness.

QUOTE

"When people start using at younger ages, the changes in brain structure and function are very, very pronounced. If we could only get kids to postpone their first drink or their first use of drugs, we could greatly diminish the prevalence of addiction in the U.S."

—Dr. John Knight, Center for Adolescent Substance Abuse Research

GLOSSARY

ADDICTION
A compulsive need for a habit-forming substance, such as nicotine or alcohol.

CHRONIC
Continuing for a long time.

DETOXIFICATION
A treatment process in which a person with a drug addiction abstains from taking a drug and doctors administer medications to help the individual's body adjust to not having the drug.

EPIDEMIC
The widespread occurrence of something negative.

INFECTIOUS
Able to be transmitted from one person to another.

NEUROTRANSMITTER
A brain chemical that helps brain cells communicate with other brain cells.

OPIOID
A class of drugs that act on the central nervous system to relieve pain.

RELAPSE
A recurrence of a disease or other ailment after it seems to have been conquered or cured.

SOBRIETY
The state of being sober; not under the influence of alcohol or mind-altering drugs.

STIGMA
A mark of disgrace or a set of negative beliefs society holds about a particular group, such as people with drug addictions or people with mental illness.

VACCINE
A drug that prevents or treats illness by stimulating the immune system to create antibodies or by blocking the effects of a substance.

ADDITIONAL RESOURCES

SELECTED BIBLIOGRAPHY

"Facing Addiction in America." *Surgeon General*. US Department of Health & Human Services, n.d. Web. 19 Sept. 2017.

Korry, Elaine. "To Prevent Addiction in Adults, Help Teens Learn How to Cope." *NPR*. NPR, 12 Nov. 2015. Web. 19 Sept. 2017.

Lewis, Marc D. *The Biology of Desire*. New York: PublicAffairs, 2015. Print.

FURTHER READINGS

Abramovitz, Melissa. *Brain Science*. Minneapolis: Abdo, 2016. Print.

Burling, Alexis. *Cocaine*. Minneapolis: Abdo, 2019. Print.

Lembke, Anna. *Drug Dealer, MD*. Baltimore, MD: Johns Hopkins UP, 2016. Print.

ONLINE RESOURCES

Booklinks
NONFICTION NETWORK
FREE! ONLINE NONFICTION RESOURCES

To learn more about heroin and prescription opioids, visit **abdobooklinks.com.** These links are routinely monitored and updated to provide the most current information available.

MORE INFORMATION

For more information on this subject, contact or visit the following organizations:

CENTERS FOR DISEASE CONTROL AND PREVENTION
1600 Clifton Road
Atlanta, GA 30329-4027
800-232-4636
cdc.gov

The Centers for Disease Control and Prevention tracks health and illness statistics in the United States and offers extensive information on trends, research, and specific diseases.

THE NATIONAL CENTER ON ADDICTION AND SUBSTANCE ABUSE
633 Third Avenue, 19th Floor
New York, NY 10017-6706
212-841-5200
centeronaddiction.org

The National Center on Addiction and Substance Abuse is a nonprofit organization that provides information about how to prevent and treat various types of drug addiction.

SUBSTANCE ABUSE AND MENTAL HEALTH SERVICES ADMINISTRATION
5600 Fishers Lane
Rockville, MD 20857
1-877-726-4727
samhsa.gov

SAMHSA is an agency within the US Department of Health and Human Services that leads efforts to reduce the impact of drug addiction and mental illness on communities.

SOURCE NOTES

CHAPTER 1. KATIE'S STORY

1. Taylor Langston. "Parents of Plant High Cheerleader Urge Others to Learn from Her Death by Heroin Overdose." *Tampa Bay Times*. Tampa Bay Times, 26 July 2017. Web. 1 Dec. 2017.

2. "Opioid Addiction." *American Society of Addiction Medicine*. American Society of Addiction Medicine, n.d. Web. 1 Dec. 2017.

3. The President's Commission on Combating Drug Addiction and the Opioid Crisis. "Draft." *White House*. White House, n.d. Web. 1 Dec. 2017.

4. Laura Harris. "Parents of Plant High School Student Who Died of Heroin Use Now Meeting with State Attorney." *ABC Action News*. E. W. Scripps, 30 Aug. 2017. Web. 1 Dec. 2017.

5. Lindsey Bever. "'How Did This Happen to a 10-Year-Old?': Child Dies with Heroin and Fentanyl in His System." *Washington Post*. Washington Post, 18 July 2017. Web. 1 Dec. 2017.

6. Emily de La Bruyère. "Middletown, Ohio, a City Under Siege: 'Everyone I Know Is on Heroin.'" *Yahoo*. Yahoo, 2 Aug. 2017. Web. 1 Dec. 2017.

7. Sam Quinones. *Dreamland*. New York: Bloomsbury, 2016. Print.

8. Julie Turkewitz. "'The Pills Are Everywhere': How the Opioid Crisis Claims Its Youngest Victims." *New York Times*. New York Times Company, 20 Sept. 2017. Web. 1 Dec. 2017.

9. "Results from the 2016 National Survey on Drug Use and Health: Detailed Tables." *SAMHSA*. SAMHSA, n.d. Web. 1 Dec. 2017.

CHAPTER 2. WHAT ARE OPIOIDS?

1. "The History of Heroin." *Heroin.net*. Heroin.net, n.d. Web. 1 Dec. 2017.

2. "Heroin." *CESAR*. University of Maryland, n.d. Web. 1 Dec. 2017.

CHAPTER 3. IMPACTS ON THE BRAIN AND BODY

1. Richard F. Thompson. *The Brain: A Neuroscience Primer*. New York: Freeman, 2000. Print. 162.

2. Elaine Korry. "To Prevent Addiction in Adults, Help Teens Learn How To Cope." *NPR*. NPR, 12 Nov. 2015. Web. 1 Dec. 2017.

3. "Drugs, Brains, and Behavior: The Science of Addiction." *National Institute on Drug Abuse*. National Institute on Drug Abuse, n.d. Web. 1 Dec. 2017.

4. Joseph C. Mancini. *Heroin Death*. Scottsdale, AZ: Bellisimo, 2017. Print. 23.

5. Mancini, *Heroin Death*, 20.

6. "Heroin Overdose Data." *CDC*. US Department of Health & Human Services, n.d. Web. 1 Dec. 2017.

CHAPTER 4. RISKS AND EFFECTS

1. Julia Conley. "Women and the Opioid Epidemic." *A Woman's Thing*. A Woman's Thing, 8 Aug. 2017. Web. 1 Dec. 2017.

2. "Heroin Addiction: 'I Needed the Drug Just to Get By.'" *National Institute on Drug Abuse*. National Institute on Drug Abuse, n.d. Web. 1 Dec. 2017.

3. Gabor Maté. *In the Realm of Hungry Ghosts*. Berkeley, CA: North Atlantic, 2010. Print. 29–30.

4. B. P. Smyth, et al. "Lapse and Relapse Following Inpatient Treatment of Opiate Dependence." *Irish Medical Journal* 103.6 (2010). Web. 1 Dec. 2017.

5. Lance M. Dodes. *The Heart of Addiction*. New York: HarperCollins, 2002. Print. 73.

6. "Opioid Addiction." *American Society of Addiction Medicine*. American Society of Addiction Medicine, n.d. Web. 1 Dec. 2017.

7. Maté, *In the Realm of Hungry Ghosts*, 296.

8. Tracey Helton Mitchell. *The Big Fix*. Berkeley, CA: Seal, 2016. Print. 5.

9. "The Science of Drug Abuse and Addiction: The Basics." *National Institute on Drug Abuse*. National Institute on Drug Abuse, n.d. Web. 1 Dec. 2017.

10. "Addiction as a Disease." *National Center on Addiction and Substance Abuse*. National Center on Addiction and Substance Abuse, n.d. Web. 1 Dec. 2017.

11. Marc Lewis. *The Biology of Desire*. New York: Public Affairs, 2015. Print. xiii.

12. Maia Szalavitz. "Most of Us Still Don't Get It: Addiction Is a Learning Disorder." *Substance.com*. Substance.com, 17 July 2017. Web. 1 Dec. 2017.

13. Mitchell, *The Big Fix*, 188.

CHAPTER 5. SOCIAL EFFECTS

1. Sam Quinones. *Dreamland*. New York: Bloomsbury, 2016. Print. 18–26.

2. "Drug Overdose Death Data." *CDC*. US Department of Health & Human Services, n.d. Web. 1 Dec. 2017.

3. Emily de La Bruyère. "For Taxpayers, the Drug Epidemic's Bills Come Due." *Yahoo*. Yahoo, 2 Aug. 2017. Web. 1 Dec. 2017.

4. Emily de La Bruyère. "Middletown, Ohio, a City Under Siege: 'Everyone I Know Is on Heroin.'" *Yahoo*. Yahoo, 2 Aug. 2017. Web. 1 Dec. 2017.

5. de La Bruyère, "Middletown, Ohio, a City Under Siege."

6. Emily Gee and Richard G. Frank. "Senate's Opioid Fund Cannot Substitute for Health Coverage." *Center for American Progress*. Center for American Progress, 20 June 2017. Web. 1 Dec. 2017.

7. de La Bruyère, "For Taxpayers, the Drug Epidemic's Bills Come Due."

8. Jean Y. Ko, et al. "Incidence of Neonatal Abstinence Syndrome—28 States, 1999–2013." *CDC*. US Department of Health & Human Services, 12 Aug. 2016. Web. 1 Dec. 2017.

9. "The Opioid Epidemic's Toll on Pregnant Women and Their Babies." *WNYC*. New York Public Radio, 9 Jan. 2016. Web. 1 Dec. 2017.

10. "The Problem of Neonatal Abstinence Syndrome." *CDC*. US Department of Health & Human Services, n.d. Web. 20 Aug. 2017.

11. "The Problem of Neonatal Abstinence Syndrome."

CHAPTER 6. THE OPIOID EPIDEMIC

1. T. J. Cicero, et al. "The Changing Face of Heroin Use in the United States: A Retrospective Analysis of the Past 50 Years." *JAMA Psychiatry* 71.7 (2014). Web. 1 Dec. 2017.

2. "Opioid Addiction." *American Society of Addiction Medicine*. American Society of Addiction Medicine, n.d. Web. 1 Dec. 2017.

3. Sam Quinones. *Dreamland*. New York: Bloomsbury, 2016. Print. 126.

4. "Statement of Purdue Pharma L.P. Regarding FDA's Approval of Reformulation of OxyContin (Oxycodone HCL Controlled-Release) Tablets." *Purdue*. Purdue Pharma, 5 Apr. 2010. Web. 1 Dec. 2017.

SOURCE NOTES CONTINUED

5. Abby Alpert, David Powell, and Rosalie Liccardo Pacula. "Supply-Side Drug Policy in the Presence of Substitutes: Evidence from the Introduction of Abuse-Deterrent Opioids." *National Bureau of Economic Research*. National Bureau of Economic Research, Jan. 2017. Web. 1 Dec. 2017.

6. Quinones, *Dreamland*, 165.

7. Todd C. Frankel. "Pellets, Planes, and the New Frontier." *Washington Post*. Washington Post, 24 Sept. 2015. Web. 1 Dec. 2017.

8. Quinones, *Dreamland*, 147.

9. Quinones, *Dreamland*, 192.

10. Wilson M. Compton, et al. "Relationship between Nonmedical Prescription-Opioid Use and Heroin Use." *New England Journal of Medicine* 374 (2016). Web. 1 Dec. 2017.

11. Quinones, *Dreamland*, 43.

12. Nadia Kounang. "Lawsuit Alleges That NFL Teams Gave Painkillers Recklessly." *CNN*. Cable News Network, 13 Mar. 2017. Web. 1 Dec. 2017.

CHAPTER 7. STIGMA AND DRUG ABUSE

1. Lauren Villa. "Shaming the Sick: Addiction and Stigma." *DrugAbuse.com*. DrugAbuse.com, n.d. Web. 1 Dec. 2017.

2. David T. Courtwright. "A Century of American Narcotic Policy." *Treating Drug Problems* 2 (1992). Web. 1 Dec. 2017.

3. Courtwright, "A Century of American Narcotic Policy."

4. Sam Quinones. *Dreamland*. New York: Bloomsbury, 2016. Print. 54.

5. "Drugs, Brains, and Behavior: The Science of Addiction." *National Institute on Drug Abuse*. National Institute on Drug Abuse, n.d. Web. 1 Dec. 2017.

6. Akikur Mohammad. *The Anatomy of Addiction*. New York: Perigee, 2016. Print. 4.

7. Max Blau. "STAT Forecast: Opioids Could Kill Nearly 500,000 Americans in the Next Decade." *STAT*. STAT, 27 June 2017. Web. 1 Dec. 2017.

8. Colleen L. Barry, et al. "Stigma, Discrimination, Treatment Effectiveness and Policy Support: Comparing Public Views about Drug Addiction with Mental Illness." *Psychiatric Services* 65.10 (2014). Web. 1 Dec. 2017.

9. Shari Rudavsky. "They Live with Chronic Pain. They're Treated Like Addicts," *IndyStar*. IndyStar, 5 Nov. 2017. Web. 1 Dec. 2017.

10. Villa, "Shaming the Sick: Addiction and Stigma."

11. Alana Levinson. "Surviving the Secret Childhood Trauma of a Parent's Drug Addiction." *Pacific Standard*. Social Justice Foundation, 20 Nov. 2014. Web. 1 Dec. 2017.

12. Tracey Helton Mitchell. *The Big Fix*. Berkeley, CA: Seal, 2016. Print. 12.

13. Claire Rudy Foster. "The Stigma of Addiction Is More Dangerous Than Drug Overdoses." *Huffpost*. Oath, 14 July 2017. Web. 1 Dec. 2017.

14. Chris York. "Parent's Heroin Overdose Pictures with Child in Car Released by Ohio Police." *Huffpost*. Oath, 9 Oct. 2016. Web. 1 Dec. 2017.

15. Joan Trujols. "The Brain Disease Model of Addiction: Challenging or Reinforcing Stigma?" *Lancet*. Elsevier, Apr. 2015. Web. 1 Dec. 2017.

CHAPTER 8. PREVENTION AND TREATMENT

1. "Prevention of Substance Abuse and Mental Illness." *SAMHSA*. SAMHSA, n.d. Web. 1 Dec. 2017.

2. Akikur Mohammad. *The Anatomy of Addiction*. New York: Perigee, 2016. Print. ix–xi.

3. Mohammad, *The Anatomy of Addiction*, 11.

4. "Addiction Medicine: Closing the Gap Between Science and Practice." *National Center on Addiction and Substance Abuse*. National Center on Addiction and Substance Abuse, June 2012. Web. 1 Dec. 2017.

5. Alix Spiegel. "What Vietnam Taught Us about Breaking Bad Habits." *NPR*. NPR, 2 Jan. 2012. Web. 1 Dec. 2017.

6. Spiegel, "What Vietnam Taught Us."

7 "Methadone Treatment Issues." *California Society of Addiction Medicine*. California Society of Addiction Medicine, n.d. Web. 1 Dec. 2017.

8. Joseph C. Mancini. *Heroin Death*. Scottsdale, AZ: Bellisimo, 2017. Print. 34.

9. Drew Pinsky. *Cracked*. New York: HarperCollins, 2003. Print. 267.

10. Marc Lewis. *The Biology of Desire*. New York: Public Affairs, 2015. Print. 115.

CHAPTER 9. LAWS AND POLICIES

1. Aaron Blake. "Trump Flubs Another Promise. Declaring the Opioid Crisis a 'National Emergency.'" *Washington Post*. Washington Post, 26 Oct. 2017. Web. 12 Jan. 2018.

2. The President's Commission on Combating Drug Addiction and the Opioid Crisis. "Draft." *White House*. White House, n.d. Web. 1 Dec. 2017.

3. Newton Lee. *Counterterrorism and Cybersecurity: Total Information Awareness*. New York, Springer, 2014. Print. 46.

4. Christopher J. Ruhm. "Geographic Variation in Opioid and Heroin Involved Mortality Rates." *American Journal of Preventive Medicine*. Elsevier, 7 Aug. 2017. Web. 1 Dec. 2017.

5. "Weighing the Charges: Simple Possession of Drugs in the Federal Criminal Justice System." *United States Sentencing Commission*. Office of Public Affairs, Sept. 2016. Web. 1 Dec. 2017.

6. Samuel Oakford. "Portugal's Example: What Happened after It Decriminalized All Drugs, from Weed to Heroin." *Vice News*. Vice News, 19 Apr. 2016. Web. 1 Dec. 2017.

7. "Drug Dealing and Drug Sales Charges." *FindLaw*. Thomson Reuters, n.d. Web. 1 Dec. 2017.

8. "Drug Dealing and Drug Sales Charges."

9. "Heroin Trafficking Offenses." *United States Sentencing Commission*. Office of Public Affairs, n.d. Web. 1 Dec. 2017.

10. "Drug Dealing and Drug Sales Charges."

11. James Gray. *Why Our Drug Laws Have Failed and What We Can Do about It*. Philadelphia, PA: Temple UP, 2012. Print. 9.

12. Deborah C. England. "Selling OxyContin/Oxycodone: Penalties, Laws, and Defense." *Criminal Defense Lawyer*. Nolo, n.d. Web. 1 Dec. 2017.

13. Joel Achenbach, John Wagner, and Lenny Bernstein. "Trump Says Opioid Crisis Is a National Emergency, Pledges More Money and Attention." *Washington Post*. Washington Post, 10 Aug. 2017. Web. 1 Dec. 2017.

14. Sam Quinones. *Dreamland*. New York: Bloomsbury, 2016. Print. 353.

INDEX

ABOUT THE AUTHOR

Melissa Abramovitz is an award-winning author who specializes in writing educational nonfiction books and magazine articles for all age groups. She also writes short stories, poems, and picture books. Abramovitz graduated from the University of California, San Diego, with a degree in psychology and is also a graduate of the Institute of Children's Literature.